SISTERS OF NIA

A Cultural Enrichment Program to Empower African American Girls

D1603917

Faye Z. Belgrave | Valerie Rawls Cherry | Deborah S. Butler | Tiffany G. Townsend

Research Press ◈ 2612 North Mattis Avenue ◈ Champaign, Illinois 61822 ◈ (800) 519-2707
www.researchpress.com

Composition by Jeff Helgesen
Cover design by Linda Brown, Positive I.D. Graphic Design
Printed by McNaughton & Gunn, Inc.

ISBN 978-0-87822-606-1
Library of Congress Control Number 2008928331

Contents

Contents

Acknowledgments

Several individuals contributed to the development of this manual. The initial prototype was developed by a team headed by Dr. Valerie Cherry, at the Progressive Life Center in Washington, D.C., and included Jerveada Dixon-Addison, Linda Clark, and Dr. Dominque Charlot-Swilley. Several individuals at Virginia Commonwealth University implemented this curriculum under the leadership of Deborah Butler. The implementation team included Renee Alleyne, Anne Arnason, Crystal Awkward, Cheryl Bennett, Kim Boyd, Renee Childs, Tashundra Coard, Maya Corneille, Keneisha Dandridge, Lorraine Edwards, Susie Farag, Tamika Gilreath, Christina Grange, Vonnie Hedgepeth, Monica Jones, Wehmah Jones, Demetria Logan, Stephanie McIntosh, Olufunke Owolabi, Jerlyn Porter, Melba Reed, Angela Snead, Fay Stith, Tiamba Wilkerson, and Veleska Wyatt.

Drs. Kevin Allison, Laura Plybon, and Melba Reed, members of the evaluation team, provided continual feedback on the success of implementation and outcomes efforts. Administrative support was provided by Julia Foster-Woodson, Freida McNeil, and Vivian Lucas. Tenea Johnson served as the editor for the original manuscript, and Karen Wilson, Terence Wiles, and Fay Stith provided editorial assistance.

Individuals within several agencies worked with us in Washington, D.C., and Richmond, Virginia. Participating agencies included the Greater Southeast Head Start Program in Washington, D.C.; Washington, D.C., Public Schools; Richmond Public Schools; and the Richmond Metro area Boys and Girls Clubs.

The implementation of our curriculum was supported by grants from the U.S. Department of Health and Human Services, Substance Abuse and Mental Health Services Administration, Center for Substance Abuse Prevention. We appreciate the help of Frances Johnson, Jeanne DiLoreto, and other project officers who encouraged and supported our efforts.

Finally, we would like to thank all of the girls who enthusiastically participated in our program in Washington, D.C., and Richmond, Virginia, and their parents, who entrusted their daughters to us.

Introduction

Many African American preadolescent and adolescent girls face challenges linked to residing in low-income and low-resource communities. Some risk factors include low academic achievement and life-course expectations. Other factors include early and risky sexual behavior, sometimes resulting in unplanned pregnancy or sexually transmitted diseases. Although African American adolescent females are more likely to be exposed to drugs and related problems in their community, they are no more likely to use drugs than girls in other ethnic groups, and many of these girls show strengths, including high self-esteem, positive relationships with adults, spiritual connectedness, independence, and androgynous gender roles.

The *Sisters of Nia* program is aimed at reinforcing and bringing out the strengths of African American girls. In the Kiswahili (Swahili) language, the word *nia* means purpose or goal. Many African American girls have high goals, but they may not know how to achieve them. They may not be able to connect their current behaviors or the behaviors of those around them with their future goals. *Sisters of Nia* seeks to bridge this divide. Studies have shown that culturally relevant intervention programs can give these girls help in achieving the direction, relationship skills, identity empowerment, and critical consciousness that lead to more positive self-esteem and relationships with others, greater ethnic pride, and higher expectations for future accomplishments. Research support for the *Sisters of Nia* program is provided in Appendix A, at the back of this book.

This curriculum is for preadolescent and adolescent girls ages 10 to 14, at the stage when developmental changes coincide with other transitions—specifically, the transitions from elementary to middle school and from middle to high school. At these points in their lives, girls' goals, behaviors, and personalities are in transition—not just their bodies. They are in the process of learning from their environment how to be women.

The *Sisters of Nia* program is a supplemental environment from which young African American women can learn. The program serves as a rite of passage that complements other efforts within the family, school, or community. Specifically, the program's objectives are as follows:

- To increase knowledge of and appreciation for African and African American culture
- To increase ethnic pride and identity
- To increase identification with and awareness of successful African American female role models
- To develop critical awareness and skills for analyzing community and media messages
- To increase positive peer relationships and to decrease negative peer interactions
- To increase leadership skills and creativity
- To increase appreciation for the diversity of physical beauty and attractiveness
- To increase knowledge about personal hygiene and health
- To increase life-course expectations regarding education and other achievements

To accomplish these objectives, the program helps participants do the following:

- Learn about and from successful African American female role models
- Learn about and participate in African cultural activities and traditions
- Become aware of racism and sexism and how to deal with these "isms" in community and media messages
- Become aware of negative behaviors and the consequences of such behaviors

- Engage in role-play and team-building activities and exercises designed to promote positive relationships with other females
- Learn the Eight Principles for African American Living (*Nguzo Nane*) and discover how these principles can be applied to one's functioning in everyday life in the home, school, and community

Effective mentoring and cultural socialization can play a crucial role in positively affecting girls' lives. In implementing the program and helping to create "Sisters of Purpose," you will become one yourself. Take the time to thoroughly learn and understand the curriculum. Become familiar with its Africentric and relational principles and methods, effective teaching strategies, and session content and format. Make sure that materials are prepared and that you and your fellow leaders work cooperatively. Your ability to work well as a team and as individuals will dictate the program's success. Finally, take time to enjoy the important work you are doing.

FACILITATOR'S GUIDE

CURRICULUM OVERVIEW

The *Sisters of Nia* curriculum is a 14-week cultural enrichment program designed to encourage African American preadolescent and adolescent girls, ages 10 to 14, to develop behaviors, critical consciousness, and self-respect. Although the curriculum is designed with African American girls in mind, it can lead to greater emotional maturity and more positive relationships in any girl open to its Africentric and relational principles and group structure. Participants are organized into *jamaas,* or groups, of no more than 12 girls each. A *mzee,* or respected elder, in this case female, facilitates each *jamaa.* Each *mzee* is responsible for working as a member of the program's facilitating team, as well as for leading each two-hour session of her *jamaa.*

The Seven Principles of Kwanzaa *(Nguzo Saba),* plus an eighth principle—the principle of *Heshema,* or respect—provide the framework for the sessions. These seven principles, developed by Maulana Karenga in 1966 as a celebration of African American heritage, coupled with African community-building methods, act as program themes and lessons. In fact, the whole program is based on the principle of *nia,* or purpose, and aims to help the girls become "Sisters of Purpose." Through discussion, guest speakers, trust and confidence-building activities, journaling, and application of the lessons outside of the program space, the girls explore and integrate these principles into their own lives and so move toward this goal. In keeping with the Africentric focus, the program integrates a number of words from the Kiswahili language. These words are defined as they appear; in addition, a glossary, including phonetic pronunciations, appears at the back of this book.

Africentric and Relational Principles and Methods

In traditional African families, raising children and shepherding them through rites of passage are communal responsibilities—thus the popular saying "It takes a village to raise a child." *Sisters of Nia* adopts and adapts this philosophy for girls growing up here in the United States, where a communal way of life is dwindling, if not largely lost. As such, the program employs structural and teaching strategies that focus on both community and individual responsibility. These elements include *mzees, jamaas,* the *durara umoja, tambiko,* the call and response, the *Nguzo Nane,* and sessions about African history and culture.

The program's *mzees,* or leaders, are modeled on their traditional counterparts. *Mzees* not only act as facilitators for each session, just as they do in traditional African culture, they also serve as accessible models for the girls. Each *mzee* works with an assigned group of girls called a *jamaa,* or family. Each *jamaa* selects as a name the name of an African nation or a Kiswahili term and, in that naming, becomes a small community of individuals responsible for one another's well-being.

The *durara umoja* (unity circle) and *tambiko* (libations) are key rituals performed in each session. The *mzees* and participants (as well as any guest speakers who are present) form the *durara umoja* at the beginning and end of each session. This reminds the girls that they are not only members of their *jamaa* but also members of the larger *Sisters of Nia* community and the world beyond. Libations, or *tambiko,* are poured in honor of the ancestors at the beginning of each session. In the *Sisters of Nia* program, *tambiko* usually take the form of water poured on the soil of a plant to symbolize the renewal of life that comes with honoring the ancestors. It is believed that so long as we speak the names of our ancestors, they will never be lost to us.

Mzees use the call and response method to gather the *jamaas* together for the *durara umoja* or at any other time everyone's attention is needed. In the call and response, a mzee calls out an agreed-upon word or phrase, to which the entire group calls out an agreed-upon response. (Military cadences are somewhat similar.) In our groups, we have used the term *agoo,* and the girls reply, *amee. Agoo* means, roughly, "Attention" and *amee* is the acknowledgment, "I'm listening." These words are from the Twi language of the Akan people of Ghana, West Africa.

Each session is built on one or more of the following Eight Principles for African American Living (*Nguzo Nane):*

1. *Umoja:* Unity
2. *Kujichagulia:* Self-Determination
3. *Ujima:* Collective Work and Responsibility (Teamwork)
4. *Ujamaa:* Cooperative Economics
5. *Nia:* Purpose
6. *Kuumba:* Creativity

7. *Imani:* Faith

8. *Heshema:* Respect

Two of the 14 sessions are dedicated to African history and culture. In these sessions, the girls face their own misconceptions and misinformation about the continent. This faulty knowledge is then replaced with reliable information about African history and culture, with a special emphasis on some of Africa's historical queens and leaders.

In addition to its Africentric focus, a central feature of the program is its relational nature. Interpersonal relationships and connections are primary to the development of identity in girls. The curriculum seeks to provide a structure that promotes and nourishes positive interpersonal relationships between peers and adults. Our expectation is that the attitudes and skills associated with these positive relationships will extend beyond the program to the domains of home, school, and community.

Session Topics

Session 1: Orientation

This session introduces girls to the program, allows *mzees* and participants to get to know one another, familiarizes girls with the *Sisters of Nia* creed, and introduces girls to the call and response method.

Session 2: Jamaa Building

This session explains the purpose of the *jamaas,* creates the individual *jamaas,* allows the girls to name their *jamaa,* begins establishing an emotionally safe atmosphere within each *jamaa,* allows the girls to establish rules for their *jamaa,* and helps develop girls' understanding of the African principles for living with the introduction of the first principle.

Nguzo/Principle: Nia (Purpose)

Session 3: Introduction to Relationships

This session helps participants understand relationships, begin to develop positive relationships within the group, and start to develop team-building skills.

Nguzo/Principle: Ujima (Collective Work and Responsibility / Teamwork)

Session 4: More about Relationships

This session increases *jamaa* cohesion, continues building healthy relationships and trust within the *jamaas,* and builds on the concept of the "sister-friend."

Nguzo/Principles: Ujima (Collective Work and Responsibility / Teamwork) and Umoja (Unity)

Session 5: Africa — Fact and Fiction
Session 6: Africa — Yesterday and Today

These two sessions increase knowledge and appreciation of Africa and its culture, correct stereotypes of Africa and African people, and help girls see their connection to Africa.

Nguzo/Principle: Kujichagulia (Self-Determination)

Session 7: Mirror, Mirror: What Do You Reflect? (Part 1)

This session examines why people put down others, provides an opportunity for a discussion of judging others, and offers an opportunity for open discussion about perceptions of beauty based on skin color and hair texture.

Nguzo/Principle: Heshema (Respect)

Session 8: Mirror, Mirror: What Do You Reflect? (Part 2)

This session continues discussion of what is considered attractive, examines what can be done about put-downs, helps girls gain an understanding of how perceptions of beauty affect self-esteem, and increases girls' awareness of different kinds of beauty.

Nguzo/Principle: Heshema (Respect)

Session 9: Taking Care of Yourself — Good Hygiene and Health

This session increases knowledge about personal hygiene, encourages good hygiene, and helps girls to understand the connection between good hygiene and good health.

Nguzo/Principle: Nia (Purpose)

Session 10: Analyzing Media Messages

This session familiarizes girls with ways the media portray African American females, shows girls how to examine media messages critically, and supports girls' understanding of healthy relationships.

Nguzo/Principle: Kujichagulia (Self-Determination)

Session 11: Creativity—What I Can Offer

This session helps girls identify their leadership and creative thinking skills and encourages bonds between girls from different *jamaas*.

Nguzo/Principle: Kuumba (Creativity)

Session 12: African American Women in Leadership

This session introduces girls to African American women leaders, helps girls identify and examine their leadership qualities, and develops team-building skills.

Nguzo/Principles: Ujamaa (Cooperative Economics) and Nia (Purpose)

Session 13: Education for Life

This session increases girls' understanding of the importance of education and cultivation of knowledge, discusses education's importance in African American advancement, and helps girls consider the long-term consequences of undervaluing education.

Nguzo/Principle: Nia (Purpose)

Session 14: Faith and Closing Ceremony

This final session helps girls understand faith's role in achieving success, gives girls an opportunity to share their positive impressions of one another and the *mzees,* and recognizes participants' achievement in a closing ceremony.

Nguzo/Principle: Imani (Faith)

Optional Session: Kwanzaa

If it is the appropriate time of year, you can introduce participants to—or reinforce their knowledge of—the Kwanzaa celebration.

This session offers girls the opportunity to learn the history and symbolism of the holiday, lets them know that the holiday does not replace Christmas or Hanukkah, builds *jamaa* unity, and allows the girls to express their creativity.

Suggested Field Trip

If funds and time are available, plan an outing with your girls— hiking a trail, taking a nature walk, canoeing, or a similar activity. These activities build confidence, further develop unity, and may introduce the girls to a previously unknown talent, stress reducer, or interest.

SETTING UP THE PROGRAM

This program can be run as an after-school program in schools, churches, or community centers, or it can be conducted in any other available space in which adult supervision and desire exist. It can be used as a stand-alone curriculum or in conjunction with other programs, such as those devoted to academic tutoring or substance abuse prevention. A group or program wishing to set up a *Sisters of Nia* program will need to recruit participants, identify and train *mzees,* invite guest speakers, obtain the necessary materials for each session, and arrange for space to hold the meetings. The following discussion suggests some ways to accomplish these tasks.

Community Resources

Volunteers make the *Sisters of Nia* program possible; therefore, people are your first priority. Local colleges and universities, civic and volunteer organizations, sororities, the local chapter of the NAACP, churches, and community centers are good places to look for help. If you are seeking material donations, check with local business owners who might like to contribute funds or supplies. First and foremost, be creative, aggressive, and diligent in your search for community resources. Be bold enough to ask whether people are willing to help.

Finding and Choosing Mzees

Mzees, or group leaders, are integral to the program. They facilitate the groups and act as models for participants. Therefore, finding and choosing appropriate *mzees* is one of the most important tasks in creating a successful *Sisters of Nia* program. In order to have the most productive program possible, *mzees* must possess certain characteristics. Specifically, *mzees* should be African American or other females of African ancestry (Jamaican, Afro-Brazilian, Ghanaian, Egyptian, etc.), at least seven years older than the participants, with a minimum age of 19. A *mzee* in this age range provides a clear example of what the girls can achieve in the next stage of their maturity. If still in college, *mzees* should be good students. It may also be valuable for those who have dramatically improved in school to act as *mzees*, as a mirroring technique. In such cases, the level of improvement may be more important than a high grade-point average.

One might ask, Where do I find such outstanding young ladies? The answer—all around you. Academic honor societies (Beta Club, National Honor Society, and the like), civic or volunteer organizations, churches (don't miss out on a laid-back Sunday school teacher), the local chapter of the NAACP, schools (including colleges, where students are frequently given credit for such activities), tutors, and perhaps even your own family could be good places to recruit.

Since a diverse group of girls of different stages of maturity will participate in the program, *mzees* must be patient, sociable, and punctual. Consistency, including attendance, is key. It also helps if *mzees* share at least some of the same social or economic conditions as the participants. It goes without saying that leadership qualities are also essential. Most important, *mzees* must have demonstrated values similar to those articulated by the program. These values include interest in African and African American culture, positive value for education, and commitment to improving the lives of youth.

Finally, prospective *mzees* must be able to meet the following time commitments:

- Four hours per week for the duration of the program (14 to 16 weeks, depending on the inclusion of optional Kwanzaa and field-trip activities). The four hours per week includes two and a half hours of program implementation, an hour-long staff meeting, and 30 minutes of session preparation.
- A one-time *mzee* training session. The duration of this session is at the discretion of the implementation team, but five hours is a minimum.

Sample Mzee Training Session

There are five main objectives of the mzee training session:

Objective 1: To build a cooperative foundation so that facilitators are able to work as a team

Objective 2: To educate *mzees* on development at the preadolescent and adolescent stages, with an emphasis on behavior and cognition

Objective 3: To familiarize and educate *mzees* on Africentric and relational methods

Objective 4: To provide instruction in effective group facilitation and teaching strategies

Objective 5: To offer information about the structure and strategies of the curriculum

Let these five objectives serve as your agenda for the session. Objective 1 can be realized through discussion of your reasons for implementing or participating in the program, by practicing team-building activities from the curriculum, or by doing other team-building activities.

Short presentations by guest speakers and cultural specialists (including African American educators, psychologists, counselors, and cultural studies scholars) can help you realize Objectives 2 and 3. In lieu of such speakers, the administrative staff of the program should prepare and distribute literature on this subject. Some of this literature is referenced in the suggested resources list at the back of this book. We encourage you to supplement this material with your own research and information. After reviewing the literature, have a focused discussion on the materials, evaluating their applicability to the curriculum.

To accomplish Objective 4, review the following discussion of group facilitation and teaching strategies. Enhance this discussion with some of your own experiences as an educator. Clarify how these strategies relate to the information you have just discussed. Continue to keep these strategies in mind as you move on to the fifth objective.

To realize Objective 5, hand out copies of this book and walk through the curriculum, paying particular attention to the teaching strategies, Africentric elements, and objectives for each session.

A sample *mzee* training session schedule for a one-day meeting follows. You will notice that it includes activities from the curriculum and allows *mzee* trainees to learn as they do. Please refer to Session 1 for description of activities marked with an asterisk.

Morning

9:15	Sign-in/introductions
9:45	*Durara umoja* (unity circle) and *tambiko* (libations)*
10:00	Icebreaker activity: *Sisters of Nia* Bingo or Winds Are Blowing*
10:30	Presentation by cultural specialist
11:00	Working with African American adolescent females (see suggested resources)

Afternoon

12:15	Lunch
12:45	Team-building activity (any activity selected from the curriculum)
1:15	Distribution of *Sisters of Nia* curriculum (copies of this book) and session-by-session overview
	Overview of *mzee* responsibilities
3:00	Questions and answers
	Closing remarks

Mzee Group Facilitation and Teaching Strategies

A cooperative teaching style works best for *mzees*. This style helps manage group dynamics and models positive, productive, and respectful behavior for the girls. Be supportive, objective, and nonjudgmental. Practicing nonjudgment is key during sessions in which the girls share information or opinions that you may not have anticipated. The guidelines next described expand upon the cooperative teaching style.

Be prepared

Know the session! Read through the entire curriculum first. Then, at least two days before the session, skim over it. If need be, make a few notes to keep handy during the session, but no book. No excuses.

Be yourself

As one facilitator put it, "Teens can spot a phony a mile away." And you'd better believe they're not going to be open and honest if you're not. On this same note, if you don't know the answer to a question, say so. Tell the girls that you will have the answer at the next session. Then keep your word. Doing this teaches the girls that they don't have to know everything either, but they can find out.

Be respectful

Again, be supportive, objective, and nonjudgmental. Treat the girls as you would want to be treated.

Be clear

Clarify abstract or vague language and terms. Since the *Sisters of Nia* program is Africentric, many times the girls will need clear definitions of terms. Learn this information. The glossary and suggested resources list at the back of this book are provided specifically for this purpose.

Be positive in the face of the negative

When a participant is practicing misbehavior, separate the person from the behavior. Instead of saying, "Please stop . . ." or "Don't . . ." remind the girl of what she agreed to do according to the group's rules. State this information clearly, referring to the rule.

Recognize positive behavior

If you are going to address misbehavior, you must also acknowledge positive behavior. Keeping the scale balanced shows the girls that the *mzees* are fair. It also empowers the girls to make decisions about how they want to be recognized—for positive behavior or misbehavior.

Ask open-ended questions

Open-ended questions allow girls the space to express themselves and articulate their perspectives, as opposed to merely agreeing or disagreeing with another's point of view. When brainstorming, make sure you get all responses before moving on with the session (interpreting, classifying, clarifying).

Practice active listening

Active listeners are more aware of group dynamics moment to moment. Thus, they are more able to facilitate. When implementing sessions, give the girls your full attention. Make eye contact. Paraphrase their responses and reflect their feelings. Recognize sincere replies and responses. Validate all feelings. Use open and inviting body language. Don't be afraid of silence. Sometimes it takes a moment or two for the girls to reflect on the question or to let information sink in.

Work to include all group members

Every group has a myriad of personalities. Take the time to gently engage shy or withdrawn girls. Smile. Ask them, "How do you feel about that?" or "What do you think?" On the other end of the spectrum, some girls will be very forthcoming and vocal. Make sure that everyone receives equal attention and balanced responses. Also make sure that group members speak one at a time, beginning their statements with "I."

Be consistent

The ritualistic elements of the program (like the *durara umoja* and *tambiko*) provide needed structure and reinforcement. It is also important for *mzees* to provide transitions and closure when necessary. Thank the girls for their responses and whatever else they have provided that day. Let them know in advance when you are going to end an activity.

Enlist the support of other staff

When necessary, don't be afraid to rely upon your own peers to help during a difficult session.

SESSION COMPONENTS AND MATERIALS

The session plans following this Facilitator's Guide provide specific guidelines for conducting the group meetings.

Session Components

Each session plan includes objectives, a list of necessary materials and explanation of any additional preparations that might be required, and a step-by-step description of the procedures. Sessions are structured in the following way.

Opening rituals

Opening rituals include having the group gather together to form the *durara umoja* (circle of unity) and perform the *tambiko* (libations, or pouring of water on the earth).

Jamaa work

Following the opening rituals, the girls go to their separate *jamaas* to discuss and engage in activities relating to the *nguzo* (principle) and proverb of the day. As a part of *jamaa* work, the girls receive a loose-leaf binder and pages that include questions for discussion and individual responses. These pages, which may be photocopied from Appendix B, make up the *Sisters of Nia Journal*. The girls also receive a *Staying in Focus* assignment to do before the next session.

In addition to working in their individual *jamaas*, the girls often come together to experience large-group activities involving guest speakers, team-building activities, intellectual and cooperative challenges, African and African American history and culture, and role plays.

Closing rituals

At the end of each session, the whole group comes together to re-form the *durara umoja* and to recite the *Sisters of Nia Creed*. Snacks and informal discussion among *mzees* and participants conclude the session.

Program Materials

Besides an appropriate space, willing participants, and committed program facilitators and group leaders, the *Sisters of Nia* program requires the following materials:

- A CD player and CD of African percussion music

Facilitator's Guide

- A large map of Africa
- A potted plant and pitcher to hold water for the *tambiko*
- Easel pads (one per *jamaa)*
- Poster board and markers
- Small loose-leaf binders (one per participant, to make the *Sisters of Nia Journals*)
- A three-hole punch (to drill holes in the journal pages and handouts)
- Card stock (for photocopying the *Staying in Focus* assignments)
- Paper and pencils or pens
- Snacks to serve at the end of each session

Appendix C includes full-page versions of the Sisters of Nia Creed, the Eight Principles for African American Living (*Nguzo Nane)*, and the eight individual principles. If you wish, you can recreate these pages as larger posters for display in the program space. A few additional materials are needed to conduct specific activities; these are listed with each session.

> *Before each session, the facilitating staff should meet for an hour to prepare materials and conduct any necessary administrative or implementation discussion. It is crucial that facilitators review sessions before implementation!*

SISTERS OF NIA PROGRAM AT A GLANCE

Program type

Africentric cultural enrichment for adolescent females

Objectives

- To increase knowledge of and appreciation for African and African American culture
- To increase ethnic pride and identity
- To increase identification with and awareness of successful African American female role models
- To develop critical awareness and skills for analyzing community and media messages
- To increase positive peer relationships and to decrease negative peer interactions
- To increase leadership skills and creativity
- To increase appreciation for the diversity of physical beauty and attractiveness
- To increase knowledge about personal hygiene and health
- To increase life-course expectations regarding education and other achievements

Guiding principles

The Eight Principles for African American Living (*Nguzo Nane*)

Implementation

- Stand-alone or in conjunction with a complementary program (for example, tutoring or substance abuse prevention)
- Number of sessions: 14 (plus one additional optional session)
- Session duration: 2 hours

Sisters of Nia Program (continued)

Target group

African American (or other open and interested) girls, ages 10 to 14

Group structure

At least one facilitator *(mzee)* for each group *(jamaa)* of 8 to 12 girls

Facilitator characteristics

African American females 19 years or older in good academic standing. These could include other females of African descent.

Session environment

A large room with few distractions (windowless or covered windows, no foot traffic)

Session components

Opening and closing rituals, discussion, guest speakers, team-building activities, journaling, *Staying in Focus* activities, intellectual and cooperative challenges, African and African American history and culture, and role plays

Optional activities

Field trips, Kwanzaa celebration

SESSION PLANS

SESSION 1

Orientation

OBJECTIVES

- To provide an overview of the project, including the expectations, vocabulary, structures, and rules
- To help *mzees* and participants get to know one another

MATERIALS

CD player and CD of African percussion music

Sign-in sheet

Name tags and pins to attach them (or the stick-on variety)

Water and plant for the *tambiko*

Copies of the *Sisters of Nia Bingo* handout (p. 29)

Pens or pencils

Snacks

PREPARATION

Create posters of the *Sisters of Nia Creed* and *Nguzo Nane (Eight Principles)*. Display these posters and a large map of Africa during this and all following sessions. If you wish, you can also create posters of the individual *Nguzo/Principles* for display in the larger group. Full-page examples of these materials are included in Appendix C.

PROCEDURE

Before the girls arrive, start the music.

Sign-in

As the girls arrive, have the *mzees* direct them to a table where they will sign in and make a name tag. *Mzees* not assigned to the sign-in table greet the girls. Music continues to play during this time.

Program Introduction

Once this and other sessions begin, no one is permitted to leave the room.

1. Turn off the music and ask everyone to gather and stand in a circle. Have the *mzees* spread themselves throughout the circle. (Do not hold hands at this time.)

2. Give a brief overview of the program, describing the goals, expectations for attendance, and some of the future session topics. Refer the girls to the *Nguzo Nane/Eight Principles* poster and let them know they will be learning about these principles in the program sessions.

3. Briefly explain the cultural elements of the program, describing the roles in African culture of the *mzee*, the *durara umoja*, and the *tambiko*.

   Mzee: Respected elder (in this case, group leaders)

   Durara umoja: Circle of unity (symbolizing togetherness and mutual support)

   Tambiko: Libations (pouring of water into the earth in memory of ancestors)

   Tell the girls that these words are from the Kiswhahili (Swahili) language and that they will be learning other African words as the sessions go along.

4. Answer any questions. (Participants should say their names to introduce themselves before asking a question.)

5. Introduce the call and response signal that will be used to get the group's attention. Explain that the words to be used are from the Twi language of the Akan people of Ghana, West Africa: *agoo,* which means "Attention," and *amee,* which means "I'm listening." Practice the call and response signal with the girls.

   Point out Ghana on the map of Africa.

Opening Rituals

- Instruct everyone standing in the circle to hold hands, forming the *durara umoja*. Remind the girls of the circle's purpose and significance.

- Have participants and *mzees* go around the circle to introduce themselves and share one thing for which they are thankful.

- Perform the *tambiko* by pouring the water on the plant. If you wish, you can call out the name of an African American historical figure or female ancestor (e.g., Harriet Tubman or your grandmother) before you perform the *tambiko*.

- Conduct one of the two following icebreaker activities.

Icebreaker Activities

SISTERS OF NIA BINGO

This icebreaker is a fun and informal way for the mzees and girls to get to know one another. It also gives the girls an opportunity to share something special about themselves with the entire group. You can adapt the bingo sheet according to the number of participants you have. Collect the sheets after the activity to include in the girls' journals.

Directions

1. Hand out the bingo sheets and pens or pencils. Tell the group that everyone must find people who fit the categories listed in the squares and get their signatures. Each square requires two signatures, and no one person may sign a sheet more than twice. Depending on the time available, you can stop the game after four or five people have bingo (four spaces in a line, vertically, horizontally, or diagonally).

2. Next select a category from the sheet and ask, "Who found someone who _____?" Have a participant who responds to this question read a name from her sheet. Ask the person whose name has been read to elaborate or demonstrate, depending on the category. Then, staying with the same category, ask the group: "Did anyone have someone different for

this category?" Continue until you have covered four to six categories, depending on the amount of time available.

The Wind Is Blowing

This is an energizer icebreaker. The goal is to be as inclusive as possible and to learn more about one another. It is similar to musical chairs except that no one leaves the game. Because you are getting to know the girls, it is important to use this activity as an opportunity to observe who responds to which categories to learn more about them.

Directions

1. Set up chairs in a circle. Use enough chairs for all but one participant.

2. Demonstrate how to play by standing in the center of the circle and saying, "The winds are blowing for anyone who _____." (For example: "The winds are blowing for anyone who *likes to dance*.")

3. Instruct everyone who fits the description to get up and move quickly to another chair. The person who does not find a chair goes to the center of the circle and gives the next instruction.

4. Challenge the girls to "fill in the blank" with categories that aren't visual—for example, anyone who has a pet; who occupies a certain place in the birth order (a youngest child who has an older brother, someone who has a younger sister); or who likes a certain season, color, flavor of ice cream, or pizza topping.

Closing Rituals

- Call the group to order, using the call and response method, then have participants form the *durara umoja*.

- Refer participants to the poster of the *Sisters of Nia Creed*. Have everyone recite the creed together.

  Share the snacks. Mzees may use this opportunity to chat informally with all of the girls. Afterward, encourage everyone to help with clean-up.

SISTERS OF NIA BINGO

Name _____ **Date** _____

Find people to fit the categories below and have them sign their names, one person per square. No one may sign more than twice on the same sheet.

Likes okra	Can do a cartwheel	Can speak another language	Has read a book this month
Knows how to play chess	Can wiggle their ears	Can jump rope "Double Dutch" style	Baby-sits
Sings in a choir	Plays an instrument	Can name three African countries	Has been to church this month
Plays on a sports team	Likes to cook	Was born in another state or country	Likes to draw

From *Sisters of Nia: A Cultural Program to Empower African American Girls,* © 2008 by F. Z. Belgrave, V.R. Cherry, D.S. Butler, & T.G. Townsend. Champaign, IL: Research Press (www.researchpress.com; 1–800–517–2707)

Jamaa Building: Purpose, Introductions, and Rules

OBJECTIVES

- To create individual *jamaas,* or groups, and begin to establish an emotionally safe atmosphere within them
- To begin building cohesion among participants

MATERIALS

CD player and CD of African percussion music

Water and plant for the *tambiko*

Easel pads and markers (one per *jamaa*)

Copies of the *Possible Jamaa Names* handout *(optional)*

Journals (loose-leaf binders, one per participant) and copies of the session's journal pages (Appendix B, pp. 133–135)

Pencils or pens

Session 2 *Staying in Focus* assignment cards

Snacks

PREPARATION

- Determine how many *jamaas* you will need and decide on a way to assign participants to each (see the suggested activity). Assign one or more *mzees* to each *jamaa.*
- Assemble journals for each participant, including journal pages for the session. If you wish, you can include each girl's bingo sheet from the last session as well.

PROCEDURE

Before the girls arrive, start the music. Continue to display the posters of the Nguzo Nane (Eight Principles) and Sisters of Nia Creed, along with the map of Africa.

Opening Rituals

- Turn off the music and gather everyone together for the *durara umoja*. (*Mzees* should spread themselves throughout the circle.) Ask if anyone remembers the purpose and significance of the circle. Remind the group if necessary.

- Review the purpose of and perform the *tambiko*.

Jamaa-Forming Activity

When forming jamaas, it is important to separate cliques and prevent last-minute switches as girls attempt to stay with their friends. Here is one procedure using index cards of different colors to create balanced group membership within jamaas.

- Create a stack of colored index cards based on how many *jamaas* you will need and how many girls will be in each *jamaa*. For example, if there will be three *jamaas* of eight girls each, you could use eight blue, green, and yellow cards (a total of 24). Alternate the colors—stacking first a blue card, then a green card, and finally a yellow card—until all 24 cards have been stacked.

- While the large group is still in the *durara umoja*, distribute the cards, being sure to rotate through the colors until all the cards have been given out. Girls having cards of the same color form a *jamaa*.

- Have the *mzees* collect their *jamaa* members, go to separate areas of the room, and sit in their own respective circles.

Jamaa Work

1. Circulate a sheet of paper and ask the members of your group to sign their names, then explain the purpose and function of the *jamaa*.

Jamaa: A group or family (in this case, formed to help the girls work together to become Sisters of Nia).

2. Have the group vote on a name for their *jamaa.* Ideas include having the girls choose from among the names of African nations or words on the *Possible Jamaa Names* handout.

3. Conduct an introduction exercise: Have each girl give her name and finish the following statement: "One thing I can contribute to my *jamaa* is _____." This should be a positive quality. If a participant has difficulty thinking of something, let her pass and come back to her at the end. If she continues to struggle, assist her. Make sure to reframe any negatively worded statements. For example, instead of "I won't talk over others," encourage the girl to say, " I will practice listening to others."

4. Explain the purpose of group rules or cultural norms. For example, you could say: "In life, we have rules for several reasons. Some of these reasons are to help people feel safe, to observe and preserve culture, and to create an environment where people feel respected." Give a concrete example of how a person might show respect (listening when others talk, using words instead of hurting others when we disagree).

5. Ask the group what rules they think the *jamaa* should have. Write these down on the easel pad. Tell the group that many rules are *nonnegotiable,* meaning that everyone must follow them. At minimum, the following rules need to be included:

   - Respect elders.
   - Respect one another.
   - Speak only positively about people.
   - Maintain confidentiality.
   - No fighting.

   Put an asterisk next to each necessary rule. Any remaining rules, such as "We should love each other," are optional and may be adopted on an individual basis.

6. To show their willingness to abide by the rules, have the members sign their names to the list of rules.

7. Next ask for two volunteers to write the *nguzo* and proverb of the day:

Nguzo/Principle: Nia (Purpose)

Proverb: "Before shooting, one must aim."

> *To be able to write the principle and proverb, volunteers will need something to refer to. Options for this and following sessions include giving them their journal page early and having them copy from that or preparing and giving them separate index cards (principle written on one, proverb written on the other).*

8. Have participants practice saying the *nguzo,* then ask the group to relate the proverb to the principle. You can point out that in order to accomplish something, there has to be a purpose.

9. Give each participant a journal, pen or pencil, and the journal pages for the session. Have each girl fill out the title page and answer the questions on page 135. Point out that the journal includes a copy of the *Sisters of Nia Creed* and let participants know that they will be adding pages to these journals as the sessions continue. Answer any questions.

10. Collect the journals and pencils or pens and give each girl a *Staying in Focus* assignment card. Read and discuss the instructions on the card:

    "Between now and the next session, practice two of your *jamaa's* rules in your family or at school."

    Answer any questions about the assignment and tell the girls that you want everyone to bring the card to the next session and be ready to share their answers.

Closing Rituals

-   Get the whole group's attention, using the call and response method.
-   Form the *durara umoja* and have everyone read the *Sisters of Nia Creed* aloud together.

    > *Share the snacks. Mzees chat informally with the girls. Afterward, encourage everyone to help with clean-up.*

POSSIBLE JAMAA NAMES

Word	Meaning	Language
THEMBA (TEHM-bah)	Hope	Xosa, spoken in southern Africa
AZIZA (ah-ZEE-zah)	Precious	Kiswahili, spoken in eastern Africa
RASHIDA (RAH-shee-dah)	Righteous	Kiswahili, spoken in eastern Africa
NGOZI (n-GOH-zee)	Blessing	Ibo, spoken in Nigeria
ZAWADI (zah-WAH-dee)	Gift	Kiswahili, spoken in eastern Africa
SAIDAH (SAH-ee-dah)	Happy or fortunate	Arabic, spoken in northern Africa
ZURI (ZUH-ree)	Beautiful	Kiswahili, spoken in eastern Africa
MALIKA (MAH-lee-kah)	Queen	Kiswahili, spoken in eastern Africa
AYO (AH-yo)	Great joy	Yoruba, spoken in Nigeria
SERWA (sair-WAH)	Noblewoman	Ewe, spoken in Ghana

From *Sisters of Nia: A Cultural Program to Empower African American Girls,* © 2008 by F. Z. Belgrave, V.R. Cherry, D.S. Butler, & T.G. Townsend. Champaign, IL: Research Press (www.researchpress.com; 1–800–517–2707)

STAYING IN FOCUS ASSIGNMENT CARDS

Photocopy this page on card stock, then cut the cards apart (one card per participant).

SESSION 2: STAYING IN FOCUS

Between now and the next session, practice two of your *jamaa's* rules in your family or at school.

SESSION 2: STAYING IN FOCUS

Between now and the next session, practice two of your *jamaa's* rules in your family or at school.

SESSION 2: STAYING IN FOCUS

Between now and the next session, practice two of your *jamaa's* rules in your family or at school.

SESSION 2: STAYING IN FOCUS

Between now and the next session, practice two of your *jamaa's* rules in your family or at school.

SESSION 2: STAYING IN FOCUS

Between now and the next session, practice two of your *jamaa's* rules in your family or at school.

SESSION 2: STAYING IN FOCUS

Between now and the next session, practice two of your *jamaa's* rules in your family or at school.

36

From *Sisters of Nia: A Cultural Program to Empower African American Girls,* © 2008 by F. Z. Belgrave, V.R. Cherry, D.S. Butler, & T.G. Townsend. Champaign, IL: Research Press (www.researchpress.com; 1–800–517–2707)

Introduction to Relationships

OBJECTIVES

- To help participants understand what a relationship is and identify different types of relationships
- To encourage participants to begin to develop more positive relationships

MATERIALS

CD player and CD of African percussion music

Water and plant for the *tambiko*

Easel pads and markers (one per *jamaa*)

A jump rope (heavy clothesline or rope, about 15 feet long)

Easel pad and marker for each *jamaa*

Journals and copies of the Session 3 journal page (Appendix B, p. 136)

Session 3 *Staying in Focus* assignment cards

Snacks

PROCEDURE

Before the girls arrive, start the music. Continue to display the posters of the Nguzo Nane (Eight Principles) and Sisters of Nia Creed, along with the map of Africa.

Opening Rituals

- Turn off the music and instruct everyone to hold hands, forming the *durara umoja*. (*Mzees* should spread themselves throughout the circle.) Ask the group: "What is the significance of the *durara umoja?*" If no one responds, remind participants that the circle symbolizes unity among group members.
- Review the purpose of and perform the *tambiko*.

  Instruct the girls to get out their Staying in Focus cards and go to their jamaas.

Jamaa Work

1. Ask for three volunteers. Have one volunteer post the *jamaa's* rules poster and the other two write the *nguzo* and proverb of the day:

   Nguzo/Principle: Ujima (Teamwork)

   Proverb: "Show me your friend, and I will show you your character."

2. Have the girls practice saying the *nguzo* aloud. Discuss how the *nguzo* relates to the proverb. If necessary, you can say that your friends will determine how well you work as a team.

3. Let participants know that the topic of the session will be relationships, then ask for volunteers to share their experiences doing the last session's *Staying in Focus* assignment:

   "Between now and the next session, practice two of your *jamaa's* rules in your family or at school."

   Relate the *nguzo* to the assignment to practice the rules. If necessary, you can point out that teamwork can be practiced in the home and school and that members must respect rules set up for the good of everyone in the group. When you have finished discussing, have the girls return the cards to you.

4. Next ask the girls to give a definition of *relationship*. If necessary, assist them in coming up with a broad definition—for example, a relationship is a connection between two or more people.

5. Brainstorm a list of some types of relationships. Some examples are girl-girl or "sisterhood" relationships (what the program hopes to encourage), parent-child, teacher-student,

and boy-girl. Discuss these different types of relationships. Point out that their characteristics can vary. Relationships can be warm, friendly, casual, unfriendly, and so forth.

6. Hand out the journals and pencils or pens, then give each girl a copy of the journal page for the session. Read through the page together and have the girls answer the questions. Discuss especially what makes someone a good *sister-friend*.

7. Collect the journals and pens or pencils, then give each participant a *Staying in Focus* assignment card for the session. Read and discuss the instruction on the card:

   "Between now and the next session, practice being a sister-friend to someone."

   Tell the girls that you want them to bring the card to the next session and be ready to share their answers. Encourage them to help one another remember to bring their cards back.

8. Conduct the following activity.

Team-Building Activity: Revolutions

This activity involves having the girls pass under a turning jump rope in an increasingly difficult way, thus challenging them to work together cooperatively. One way to stimulate cooperation is to limit the time to accomplish the task.

Directions

1. Clear a large space. Tell the group they are going to be given a challenge. Explain the goal and rules of the activity: Two *mzees* will serve as rope turners, and group members will pass under the jump rope, one person at a time, until the entire group is on the other side. If the rope touches anyone or goes around without someone's passing through it, the group must start over.

2. When everyone has successfully gone through one at a time, the group tries going through in pairs, threes, and so on, until finally the entire group passes as one. If there is a time constraint, announce to the group how long they have to complete the activity.

3. Ask the group if they need a few minutes to plan. Once the *mzees* begin turning the rope, the group decides when to begin.

Safety Concerns

- Rope turners should always turn the rope in the direction of the group.
- If at any time the rope comes into contact with a person, the rope turners should immediately drop their ends (this reduces the risk of someone's tripping).

Processing the Activity

- If you gave the girls a limited time to accomplish the task, ask them how it felt to know they had this limit. How did it affect their ability to communicate? To achieve success? *Stop the discussion if and when you hear scapegoating or blaming.* Ask them how this type of behavior affects the unity of the group. What can be done in place of criticizing someone?
- Close by paraphrasing the following:

  When, as a group, we try to reach a goal or complete a task and encounter problems or difficulties, the tendency is to focus on what an individual did or did not do right. When we get sidetracked into blaming and criticizing, we are no longer focusing our energy on the problem or difficulty. It is always more helpful to offer sincere suggestions on what the person *can do* than it is to point out and dwell on the mistake.

Closing Rituals

- Get the whole group's attention, using the call and response method.
- Re-form the *durara umoja* and have everyone read the *Sisters of Nia Creed* together aloud.

  Share the snacks. Mzees chat informally with all of the girls. Encourage everyone to help with clean-up.

STAYING IN FOCUS ASSIGNMENT CARDS

Photocopy this page on card stock, then cut the cards apart (one card per participant).

SESSION 3: STAYING IN FOCUS

Between now and the next session, practice being a sister-friend to someone.

SESSION 3: STAYING IN FOCUS

Between now and the next session, practice being a sister-friend to someone.

SESSION 3: STAYING IN FOCUS

Between now and the next session, practice being a sister-friend to someone.

SESSION 3: STAYING IN FOCUS

Between now and the next session, practice being a sister-friend to someone.

SESSION 3: STAYING IN FOCUS

Between now and the next session, practice being a sister-friend to someone.

SESSION 3: STAYING IN FOCUS

Between now and the next session, practice being a sister-friend to someone.

From *Sisters of Nia: A Cultural Program to Empower African American Girls*, © 2008 by F. Z. Belgrave, V.R. Cherry, D.S. Butler, & T.G. Townsend. Champaign, IL: Research Press (www.researchpress.com; 1–800–517–2707)

SESSION 4

More about Relationships

OBJECTIVES

- To increase cohesion and teamwork
- To continue building relationships and trust among group members
- To decrease any negative attitudes and behaviors girls might have toward one another

MATERIALS

CD player and CD of African percussion music

Water and plant for the *tambiko*

Easel pads and markers (one per *jamaa*)

Journals and copies of the Session 4 journal page (Appendix B, p. 137)

Pencils or pens

Session 4 *Staying in Focus* assignment cards

Snacks

PROCEDURE

Continue to display the posters of the Nguzo Nane (Eight Principles) and Sisters of Nia Creed, along with the map of Africa.

Opening Rituals

- Turn off the music. Gather everyone together for the *durara umoja*. Ask the group: "What is the significance of the *durara umoja?"* If no one responds, remind the girls that it symbolizes unity among the group.

- Perform the *tambiko.*

  Instruct the girls to get out their Staying in Focus cards and go to their jamaas.

Jamaa Work

1. Ask for three volunteers—one to post the *jamaa's* rules poster and the other two to write the principle and proverb of the day, respectively.

   Nguzo/Principles: Ujima (Teamwork) and Umoja (Unity)

   Proverb: "When spiderwebs unite, they can tie up a lion."

2. Discuss the *nguzo,* relating it to the last session's team-building activity ("Revolutions"). Encourage girls to recognize that they were dependent on one another to complete the activity.

3. Let the girls know that the session will continue the topic of relationships, then discuss the last session's *Staying in Focus* assignment:

   "Between now and the next session, practice being a sister-friend to someone."

   Ask for volunteers to share their responses. If some girls are not prepared, read the assignment to the group and solicit responses. Relate responses to the topic by telling the girls that their actions are examples of what goes into being a sister-friend and all healthy relationships. When you have finished the discussion, collect the cards.

4. On the easel pad, write down the qualities or characteristics identified in the examples the girls have shared (for example, respect, kindness, empathy, being a good listener, etc.). Expand the list by asking, "What does it mean to be a sister-friend?" Encourage the group to come up with other elements of a healthy relationship.

   You can refer back to the jamaa rules for more examples of what goes into being a sister-friend. Make sure to solicit at least one concrete example for terms such as honesty and trust.

5. Hand out the journals and pencils or pens. Give each girl a copy of the Session 4 journal page. Read through the page and ask if anyone has any questions. Have the girls complete the page.

6. Collect the journals and pens or pencils, then distribute the *Staying in Focus* assignment cards for the session:

   "Identify one thing you are doing to become a stronger sister-friend."

   Read the assignment on the card and tell the girls that you want everyone to bring their card to the next session and be ready to share their answer. Encourage them to help one another remember to bring the cards.

7. Tell the girls that by practicing honesty, kindness, peaceful problem solving, being supportive, and so forth we can all improve as sister-friends. No matter what we did yesterday or a month ago, we can start to be better sister-friends with the next activity.

Team-Building Activity: Lean on Me Circle

The goal of this activity is to build trust within the individual jamaas. This is a very high-risk activity, both emotionally and physically. If you feel that participants are not ready for this activity, you may substitute another, lower risk team-building activity.

Directions

1. Tell the group they are going to engage in a challenging activity in which the group will form a "circle of support." One person will come into the center of the circle and, when she is ready, fall gently backward into the hands of the people in the circle. The people in the circle catch her, keep her from falling, and pass her gently around the circle.

2. Paraphrase the following:

   In this activity, members of the *jamaa* will take turns practicing being supportive and encouraging. They will also take turns practicing trusting the group. This is not a competition. Because we are all individuals and unique, we react to situations differently. There is no right or wrong way to feel about this. Some people may feel excited, and some people may feel afraid. The ultimate goal of the activity is to increase the level of trust among *jamaa* members. The *jamaa* will reach this goal if they do all that they can to make the person in the center feel safe and be safe.

3. Have the group, including the *mzees*, form a circle with their shoulders touching. Explain that there are different levels of participation in the activity and not everyone needs to fall. For instance, someone can come into the circle and let everyone reach in and touch her shoulders. Another may choose to bend from the waist. Often, after seeing other group members successfully supported, these individuals may try again. The circle of support has not failed if a person chooses not to fall, provided the people in the circle have done all they can to make that person feel safe.

4. Have everyone in the circle assume the "spotter's stance." First direct everyone to take a step back with one foot. Next have them raise their hands, elbows bent and palms facing out, in front of them at approximately chest height. (Placement of the hands depends on the height of the person in the center; they should be level with or slightly below the person's shoulders.) Stress the importance of maintaining this posture and continuing to stand shoulder to shoulder as people move in and out of the circle. Tell the group that while one person is probably not strong enough to support another by herself, two or three can. (At this point, *mzees* should check the position of everyone's feet and hands and make any necessary corrections.)

5. Before a person enters the circle, she selects a "leader." The leader's responsibility is to check the safety of the circle (everyone shoulder to shoulder, one leg planted firmly behind the other, with both hands up).

6. After entering the center of the circle, the "faller" stands with her legs straight and together, arms folded across her chest and eyes closed. She checks in with her leader and, if the circle is safe, the leader gives the signal to fall.

7. The person then allows herself to fall. At all times, there should be at least two people supporting her when she is off balance.

8. A new faller and new leader are selected each time so everyone has a turn in those roles.

Safety Concerns

- Obviously, falling is the primary concern for all. It is also possible for participants to be scratched or poked in the eye. *Mzees* should remind the participant in the center to keep her arms crossed and to remain stiff. (It helps to use the example of an ironing board.) *Mzees* should also check that spotters' hands are never higher than shoulder level and should stress that, in most cases, no one person can support another by herself, but two or three people together can.

- Always have an adult who is comfortable doing so go first to model appropriate posture and demonstrate the safe way to fall. This adult should share her feelings to normalize similar feelings experienced by the girls.

- Be sure to validate the difficulty of the activity. *No one should be forced physically or badgered or teased into falling.* Some behaviors that can make members feel unsafe are jokes about falling or not catching someone, excessive laughter, threats about letting a person fall, and not providing solid physical support.

- Everyone should be gently encouraged to participate at some level; however, it is important to know that participants who have difficulty trusting others may struggle with this activity. Those who are overweight might also be reluctant to participate. Others may become fearful and mask their fear with anger, joking around, or seemingly exhibiting a lack of interest.

Processing the Activity

- After everyone has had a chance to be in the center of the circle, ask the group what it was like to take on the different roles: faller, leader, or part of the circle of support.

- Ask participants to relate their feelings about participating in the activity to being a sister-friend, teamwork, and *umoja* (unity).

Closing Rituals

- Get the whole group's attention, using the call and response method.
- Re-form the *durara umoja* and have everyone read the *Sisters of Nia Creed* together aloud.

   Share the snacks. Mzees chat informally with the girls. Encourage everyone to help with clean-up.

STAYING IN FOCUS ASSIGNMENT CARDS

Photocopy this page on card stock, then cut the cards apart (one card per participant).

SESSION 4: STAYING IN FOCUS

Identify one thing you are doing to become a stronger sister-friend.

SESSION 4: STAYING IN FOCUS

Identify one thing you are doing to become a stronger sister-friend.

SESSION 4: STAYING IN FOCUS

Identify one thing you are doing to become a stronger sister-friend.

SESSION 4: STAYING IN FOCUS

Identify one thing you are doing to become a stronger sister-friend.

SESSION 4: STAYING IN FOCUS

Identify one thing you are doing to become a stronger sister-friend.

SESSION 4: STAYING IN FOCUS

Identify one thing you are doing to become a stronger sister-friend.

From *Sisters of Nia: A Cultural Program to Empower African American Girls*, © 2008 by F. Z. Belgrave, V.R. Cherry, D.S. Butler, & T.G. Townsend. Champaign, IL: Research Press (www.researchpress.com; 1–800–517–2707)

SESSION 5

Africa: Fact and Fiction

If possible, arrange for a cultural specialist—a staff member or an invited guest—to address the group about some aspect of African culture. A travel agent or someone who has recently traveled to Africa can provide an interesting presentation.

OBJECTIVES

- To gain an understanding of girls' beliefs about and knowledge of Africa
- To identify any stereotypes girls might have about Africa and Africans
- To determine what connections girls see between Africans and African Americans

MATERIALS

CD player and CD of African percussion music

Water and plant for the *tambiko*

Easel pads and markers (one per *jamaa*)

Journals and copies of the Session 5 journal page (Appendix B, p. 138)

Pencils or pens

Session 5 *Staying in Focus* assignment cards

Snacks

PROCEDURE

Before the girls arrive, start the music. Continue to display the posters of the Nguzo Nane (Eight Principles) and Sisters of Nia Creed, along with the map of Africa.

Opening Rituals

- Turn off the music. Gather everyone together for the *durara umoja*. *Mzees* should spread themselves throughout the circle. Ask the group: "What is the significance of the *durara umoja*?" If necessary, remind the girls that it symbolizes unity among the group.
- Perform the *tambiko*.

Instruct the girls to get out their Staying in Focus cards and go to their jamaas.

Jamaa Work

1. Ask for three volunteers. Have one post the *jamaa's* rules poster and the other two write the principle and proverb of the day, respectively.

   Nguzo/Principle: Kujichagulia (Self-Determination)

   Proverb: "She who does not cultivate her fields will die of hunger."

2. Have the girls practice saying the *nguzo* aloud and discuss its meaning and relationship to the proverb. Encourage the girls to understand that each of us is responsible for what happens to us.

3. Let participants know that the session will focus on Africa, then discuss the last session's *Staying in Focus* assignment:

   "Identify one thing you are doing to become a stronger sister-friend."

   Ask for volunteers to share their responses. As they share, write these responses on the easel pad. If some girls are not prepared, read the assignment to the group and solicit responses. After the discussion, collect the cards.

4. Tell the girls that Africa is the homeland to all African Americans, just as Ireland is the homeland to Irish Americans, China is the homeland to Chinese Americans, and so forth.

5. Tell the girls that it is important as Americans of African descent to learn about Africa and that you are going take them through an exercise in their journals to see how much they know and what their thoughts are about Africa. Stress that this is a learning exercise and that they will not be graded on their responses.

6. Hand out the journals and give each girl a copy of the journal page for Session 5. Tell the girls to write a brief response to each of the statements on the page. Encourage them to work individually, be honest, and to use the first answer that comes to mind. Take them through this process quickly, without any discussion.

7. Begin discussion by asking someone to share her response to the first open-ended statement. Write it down on the easel pad. Don't allow any discussion of this first question until everyone who wants to share about the first question has had a chance to do so. Continue this process with each statement until you have completed the list. Do not allow the girls to criticize one another's statements. Validate the honesty of the responses.

> *The following discussion can take place in the individual jamaas, or you can have the jamaas reassemble and hold the discussion of responses in the larger group.*

8. To facilitate further discussion of the girls' responses, tell them that people have very different and sometimes negative attitudes about Africa. This is the case because for years, many of us have learned about Africa only from movies and television programs, which gave (and in some cases continue to portray) a very inaccurate view of Africa, one that is limited, narrow, and often racist.

9. Ask the girls, "Has the fact that we are Americans of African descent affected how we think of ourselves? Why?" Discuss their responses.

> *Possible responses may include the idea that some people may think African Americans do not work as hard as other racial or ethnic groups or that African Americans engage in more negative behaviors, such as using drugs or stealing. Others may think that kinky hair and darker skin are not as attractive as straight hair and lighter skin.*

10. After this discussion, collect the journals and pens or pencils and distribute the *Staying in Focus* assignment cards for Session 5:

"Name two countries in Africa and be prepared to say why you chose them."

Read the assignment on the card and tell the girls that you want everyone to bring their card to the next session and be ready to share their answers. Encourage them to help one another remember to bring their cards.

If you are able to arrange for a speaker, the speaker may make her presentation at this point. Allow time at the end of the presentation for questions and answers.

Closing Rituals

- Get the whole group's attention, using the call and response method.
- Re-form the *durara umoja* and have everyone read the *Sisters of Nia Creed* together aloud.

  Share the snacks. Mzees chat informally with the girls. Encourage everyone to help with clean-up.

STAYING IN FOCUS ASSIGNMENT CARDS

Photocopy this page on card stock, then cut the cards apart (one card per participant).

SESSION 5: STAYING IN FOCUS

Name two countries in Africa
and be prepared to say why you chose them.

SESSION 5: STAYING IN FOCUS

Name two countries in Africa
and be prepared to say why you chose them.

SESSION 5: STAYING IN FOCUS

Name two countries in Africa
and be prepared to say why you chose them.

SESSION 5: STAYING IN FOCUS

Name two countries in Africa
and be prepared to say why you chose them.

SESSION 5: STAYING IN FOCUS

Name two countries in Africa
and be prepared to say why you chose them.

SESSION 5: STAYING IN FOCUS

Name two countries in Africa
and be prepared to say why you chose them.

From *Sisters of Nia: A Cultural Program to Empower African American Girls*, © 2008 by F. Z. Belgrave, V.R. Cherry,
D.S. Butler, & T.G. Townsend. Champaign, IL: Research Press (www.researchpress.com; 1–800–517–2707)

Africa: Yesterday and Today

OBJECTIVES

- To increase knowledge and appreciation of Africa and African culture
- To correct stereotypes and misperceptions of Africa and African people
- To help girls realize their connection to Africa
- To contrast Africa of the past and present

MATERIALS

CD player and CD of African percussion music

Water and plant for the *tambiko*

Easel pads and markers (one per *jamaa*)

Copies of the African Queens and Leaders handout (pp. 62–64)

Journals and copies of the Session 6 journal page (Appendix B, p. 139)

Pencils or pens

Session 6 *Staying in Focus* assignment cards

Snacks

PREPARATION

Locate at least 10 photographs of modern Africa for each *jamaa*. Use personal photographs, reference books, posters from travel agencies, and other resources.

PROCEDURE

Before the girls arrive, start the music. Continue to display the posters of the Nguzo Nane (Eight Principles) and Sisters of Nia Creed, along with the map of Africa.

Opening Rituals

- Turn off the music. Gather everyone together for the *durara umoja*. *Mzees* should spread themselves throughout the circle.
- Perform the *tambiko*.

  Instruct the girls to get out their Staying in Focus assignment cards and go to their jamaas.

Jamaa Work

1. Ask for three volunteers. Have one post the *jamaa's* rules poster and the other two write the principle and proverb of the day, respectively.

   Nguzo/Principle: Kujichagulia (Self-Determination)

   Proverb: "A people without knowledge of its history is like a tree without roots."

2. Have the girls practice saying the *nguzo* aloud. Note that the *nguzo* is the same as the last session, but that the proverb is new. Discuss the meaning of the new proverb and relationship to the *nguzo*. If necessary, point out that knowing the history and culture of Africa provides African Americans with a foundation upon which to determine our own destiny.

3. Let participants know that the session will continue the topic of Africa, then discuss the last session's *Staying in Focus* assignment:

   "Name two countries in Africa and be prepared to say why you chose them."

   Ask for volunteers to share their responses, including why they chose the countries they did. As they share, write these responses on the easel pad. Ask the girls what they know about the countries they've listed and record this information as well. After the discussion, collect the cards.

If some participants are not prepared, ask the group to come up with an effective way to help each other be better prepared next week and then write down their solution.

4. Explain that many of the symbols we use in the United States today are actually of African origin. Draw an obelisk on the easel pad and ask the girls if they can think of a famous monument that resembles your drawing. (The answer is the Washington Monument.) The symbol of the healing professions, snakes around a staff, called the *caduceus*, is also taken from Africa.

5. Explain that historians call Africa the "Cradle of Civilization." Ask participants if they know why. You can point out that the earliest forms of farming, art, writing, and science were developed in Kemet, now known as Egypt, in northeast Africa. Here are some additional facts you can bring up:

   - Imhotep, who lived in ancient Egypt, is recognized as the first man of science in recorded history and the world's first doctor.

   - The greatest pyramid in the world is located in Egypt. Pyramids are huge stone structures, square at the bottom with four sides like triangles and a point at the top. The Giza Pyramid is one of the remaining seven wonders of the ancient world.

   - Hieroglyphics were the writing system of the ancient Egyptians. Symbols and pictures were used to represent words. The modern-day alphabet evolved from this system.

   - Arithmetic and other forms of mathematics were developed in Kemet and used to make statues and pyramids.

   - Al-Azhar University in Cairo, Egypt, is considered to be the oldest university in the world. It was founded roughly the same time as the city of Cairo, in 969 A.D. The first lecture was delivered in 975 A.D.

6. Give each participant a copy of the *African Queens and Leaders* handout. Ask different volunteers to read the short biographies of the queens.

   After each biography, have a *mzee* or a participant write the queen's name and a sentence identifying the queen on the easel pad. For Queen Nzingha, for example, you might write, "Angolan Queen, great military leader and diplomat. Known as the 'Amazon Queen.' " Locate the queen or leader on the map of Africa.

7. Announce to the girls that they are now going to see a different Africa than people usually see on television and in the movies. Show the girls the pictures of modern Africa and share some of the following information with them:

   - Africa is the second largest continent in land area in the world and is twice the size of the United States.

   - Africa has 53 countries in five regions: North Africa, West Africa, Central Africa, East Africa, and Southern Africa.

   - Africa has many thriving cities, with airports, modern transportation systems, high-rise buildings, businesses, cultural events, and art.

   - Although the majority of the population of Africa live in rural areas, about a third live in cities.

   - Major cities include Johannesburg, South Africa; Lagos, Nigeria; Accra, Ghana; Dakar, Senegal; Lusaka, Republic of Zambia; Nairobi, Kenya; Cairo, Egypt; and Addis-Ababa, Ethiopia.

   - Over 1,000 different languages are spoken in Africa by diverse ethnic groups, each with its own traditions, customs, and ways of life. Kiswahili is one of the more widely spoken African languages. It is spoken by more than 20 million people.

   - People in Africa practice different religions. Most people practice Christianity or Islam. Fewer people practice traditional African religions.

8. Conclude by saying that all countries have strengths and weaknesses. For example, the United States has a great deal of material wealth—a strength. On the other hand, millions of people are homeless. Ask the group some of the strengths and weaknesses of countries in Africa.

   Strengths: Rich natural resources (gold, diamonds), diverse cultures and people, strong family ties, royalty (chiefs, kings, queens), respect for elders.

Weaknesses: High rates of unemployment, poor infrastructure in some countries (roads, electricity, water systems), frequently changing governments, tribal conflict.

You can point out that the majority of countries in Africa have had independence for fewer than 50 years! Remind the girls that ALL countries have strengths and weaknesses.

9. Hand out the journals and journal page for the session and read through it together. Instruct the girls to complete the questions and, after they do so, discuss. Focus on how the girls' beliefs and attitudes about Africa have changed as a result of their participation in the last two sessions.

10. Have the girls put the *African Queens* handout in their journals. Collect the journals and pens or pencils and distribute the *Staying in Focus* assignment cards for Session 6:

"Share one new thing you've learned about Africa with someone who is not in the *Sisters of Nia* program."

Read the instruction on the card and tell the girls that you want them to bring the cards back and be ready to share their answers. Encourage them to help one another remember to bring their cards.

Closing Rituals

- Get the whole group's attention, using the call and response method.
- Re-form the *durara umoja* and have everyone read the *Sisters of Nia Creed* together aloud.

    Share the snacks. Mzees chat informally with the girls. Encourage everyone to help with clean-up.

AFRICAN QUEENS AND LEADERS

Queen Nefertiti of Kemet

—circa 1330 B.C.

In ancient Egypt, Queen Nefertiti was the wife of the Pharaoh Akenaten. Nefertiti, which means "the beautiful woman has come," is one of the most famous and beloved of all ancient Egyptians. Not much is known about where she came from or who she was. She appeared with Akhenaten during his fourth year at el-'Amarna, which was Akhenaten's new city. This new city was dedicated to the god Aten. The Egyptians held religious ceremonies celebrating Aten. Nefertiti was influential in helping her husband convert the nation of Egypt from a polytheistic (many gods) religion to a monotheistic religion (one god), dedicated to the worship of the deity Aten. The couple had six daughters. A famous bust, or sculpture of the head, of Nefertiti is now in Berlin, Germany. The bust is one of the most copied works of art.

Queen Amina of Zaria

—1536–1573

Amina was the queen of Zazzua (modern day Zaria in Nigeria). At the age of 16, Amina became the heir to her mother, Bakwa of Turunku, the ruling queen of Zazzua. With this position came responsibilities. Amina is known as the warrior queen for her military and war powers. During her reign, she expanded the domain of Zazzua to its largest size ever. She built walled forts to consolidate the territory conquered after each campaign. Some of these forts still stand today. Towns grew within these protective walls, many of which are still in existence. They are called "Ganuwar Amina," or Amina's walls.

From *Sisters of Nia: A Cultural Program to Empower African American Girls,* © 2008 by F. Z. Belgrave, V.R. Cherry, D.S. Butler, & T.G. Townsend. Champaign, IL: Research Press (www.researchpress.com; 1–800–517–2707)

Queen Nzingha of Angola

—1583–1663

Queen Nzingha came to power during the early 17th century in the kingdom of Ndongo, which is now the present-day country of Angola. She lived during a period when the Atlantic slave trade was steadily growing. This time was marked by the increased intensity of slave trading among the Portuguese. Her first major move as queen was to deliver an ultimatum to the Portuguese, demanding that they respect the terms of a treaty or else war would be declared. The Portuguese ignored her warning, and so Nzingha went to war with them, a war that lasted for many years. One of Nzingha's greatest acts as queen occurred in 1624, when she declared all territory over which she had control to be free country. This meant that all slaves who came to her country from any region would forever be free. This act makes Queen Nzingha one of the first Black nationalists.

Queen Nandi of Zululand

—1778–1826

In the year 1786, Nandi gave birth to a son, Shaka. Although the king of Zululand was overjoyed to have a son, his other wives were jealous and pressured him to send Nandi and the young boy into exile. Nandi raised her son with discipline and obedience. Steadfast and proud, she trained and guided him to be a royal heir. For her many sacrifices, Nandi was finally rewarded when her son Shaka later returned to become the greatest of all Zulu kings (Shaka Zula). To this day, Zulu people use her name, Nandi, to refer to a woman of high esteem. She is the everlasting symbol of hard work, patience, and determination.

Queen Yaa Asantewa of Ghana

—1850–1921

Queen Yaa Asantewa's fight against British colonialists is an important story in the history of Ghana. Around 1900, the British sent a governor to the city of Kumasi, the capital of Ashanti, to demand the Golden Stool, described as "the Ark of the Covenant of the Ashanti people." The Golden Stool was the supreme symbol of the sovereignty and independence for the Ashantis. Yaa

Asantewa was present at a meeting between the British governor and the Ashanti leaders. When the Ashanti kings made no reply to the British demands, she chastised them for their cowardice and said, "If you men of Ashanti will not go forward, then we women will." The Ashantis, led by Yaa Asantewa, fought bravely and gallantly. The British sent 1,400 soldiers with guns to Kumasi, eventually capturing Yaa Asantewa and other leaders and sending them into exile. Yaa Asantewa's War was the last major war led by an African woman.

President Ellen Johnson-Sirleaf (Liberia)

—1938–present

Ellen Johnson-Sirleaf was sworn in as the first female elected leader of Liberia and the first female leader of an African country. Johnson-Sirleaf graduated from the College of West Africa (Monrovia), received a bachelor's degree in accounting from the University of Wisconsin in Madison, then received a master's degree in public administration from Harvard University. She was imprisoned in the 1980s for criticizing the Liberian government of the day and was forced into exile. During the time in Liberia and in exile, she served in a number of financial positions. She served as Minister of Finance in Liberia, and while in exile in Kenya from 1983 to 1985 she served as Director of Citibank in Nairobi. On November 23, 2005, Ellen Johnson-Sirleaf was declared the winner of the Liberian election and confirmed as the country's next president. Her inauguration, attended by dignitaries such as First Lady Laura Bush and Secretary of State Condoleezza Rice, took place on January 16, 2006. She has four sons and six grandchildren.

STAYING IN FOCUS ASSIGNMENT CARDS

Photocopy this page on card stock, then cut the cards apart (one card per participant).

SESSION 6: STAYING IN FOCUS Share one new thing you've learned about Africa with someone who is not in the *Sisters of Nia* program.	**SESSION 6: STAYING IN FOCUS** Share one new thing you've learned about Africa with someone who is not in the *Sisters of Nia* program.
SESSION 6: STAYING IN FOCUS Share one new thing you've learned about Africa with someone who is not in the *Sisters of Nia* program.	**SESSION 6: STAYING IN FOCUS** Share one new thing you've learned about Africa with someone who is not in the *Sisters of Nia* program.
SESSION 6: STAYING IN FOCUS Share one new thing you've learned about Africa with someone who is not in the *Sisters of Nia* program.	**SESSION 6: STAYING IN FOCUS** Share one new thing you've learned about Africa with someone who is not in the *Sisters of Nia* program.

From *Sisters of Nia: A Cultural Program to Empower African American Girls*, © 2008 by F. Z. Belgrave, V.R. Cherry, D.S. Butler, & T.G. Townsend. Champaign, IL: Research Press (www.researchpress.com; 1–800–517–2707)

Mirror, Mirror: What Do You Reflect? (Part I)

This session involves performance of a skit about a conflict between young African American women involving skin color and hair texture.

OBJECTIVES

- To have the girls examine why people use put-downs and say negative things about others
- To provide an opportunity for an open discussion on judging others
- To discuss perceptions of beauty based on skin color and hair texture

MATERIALS

CD player and CD of African percussion music

Water and plant for the *tambiko*

Easel pads and markers (one per *jamaa*)

Journals and copies of the Session 7 journal page (Appendix B, p. 140)

Pencils or pens

A copy of the Mirror, Mirror Situations

Session 7 *Staying in Focus* assignment cards

Snacks

PREPARATION

If resources allow, enlist the help of young adults or adults to play the roles in one or more of the skits. You can also ask for volunteers from among participants. In any case, you will need to give the role players time in advance of the session to discuss and prepare the skit or skits.

PROCEDURE

Before the girls arrive, start the music. Continue to display the posters of the Nguzo Nane (Eight Principles) and Sisters of Nia Creed, along with the map of Africa.

Opening Rituals

- Turn off the music. Gather everyone together for the *durara umoja*. *Mzees* should spread themselves throughout the circle.
- Perform the *tambiko*.

Instruct the girls to get out their Staying in Focus assignment cards and go to their jamaas.

Jamaa Work

1. Ask for three volunteers. Have one post the *jamaa's* rules poster and the other two write the principle and proverb of the day, respectively.

   Nguzo/Principle: Heshema (Respect)

   Proverb: "One who defames another's character also defames her own."

2. Have the girls practice saying the *nguzo* aloud. Discuss the meaning of the *nguzo* in relationship to the proverb. If necessary, explain that when you talk negatively about others, you disrespect yourself.

3. Let participants know that the topic of the session concerns negative messages girls and women send one another about their appearance, then discuss the last session's *Staying in Focus* assignment:

   "Share one new thing you've learned about Africa with someone who is not in the *Sisters of Nia* program."

   Ask for volunteers to share their responses by telling what they shared and with whom. Write their responses on the easel pad. If more girls are prepared than in the last session, recognize their effort.

4. Next ask the girls if anyone can relate the idea of negative perceptions and stereotypes about Africa to the topic of this session. If necessary, give them a few hints to help them make the connection:

   - Remind them of the discussion of the impact of negative perceptions and stereotypes of Africa and African Americans on the self-image of African Americans, especially females.

   - Make the connection between this imposed negative self-image and a girl's or woman's perception of beauty.

   - Discuss the way in which this perception affects how some African American girls and women talk to and treat one another.

5. Conduct the following activity.

Role-Play Activity

Directions

1. Reassemble in the larger group and tell participants that they are now going to see a skit or skits showing how comments and beliefs about appearance affect some young African American women. Ask the girls to keep the topics they have just discussed in mind as they watch.

2. Conduct one or more the skits. Afterward, ask the group the following questions:

   - What do you think or feel about what you saw and heard?
   - What do you think was really going on in the situation?
   - From where does our perception of beauty come, and what influences it?
   - What is meant by "internalized racism"?
   - Have any of you had a personal problem-solving or coping experience that is relevant to the topic?
   - What can we do as individuals to bring about change in this one aspect of our lives?

---

6. Have the groups break into their individual *jamaas* again. Hand out the journals, pencils or pens, and the journal page for the session. Read through the page and have the girls discuss and answer the questions. There may be a lot of energy around this topic, so make sure that one person talks at a time and that participants use "I" statements to share their opinions.

7. Collect the journals and pencils or pens, then distribute the *Staying in Focus* assignment cards for Session 7:

"Think about what makes a person attractive."

Tell the girls that at the next session you want everyone to bring their card and be ready to share their answers. Continue to encourage the group to help one another remember to bring their cards. Point out that this is a family responsibility.

8. Validate the girls' interest in trying to get to the root of the problem of putting down and stereotyping each other based on hair texture and skin color. You can paraphrase the following:

> For more than 300 years, African American women have lived in a dominant culture that labels many of our physical features as ugly and unattractive. This is true even today. It is not so surprising, then, that we are so judgmental of our physical appearance.

Tell participants that at the next session they will have a chance to talk about what they can do to improve the situation.

Closing Rituals

- Get the whole group's attention, using the call and response method.
- Re-form the *durara umoja* and have everyone read the *Sisters of Nia Creed* together aloud.

    Share the snacks. Mzees chat informally with the girls. Encourage everyone to help with clean-up.

MIRROR, MIRROR SITUATIONS

Situation 1

Two African American girls with light skin are standing by their lockers talking when one sees a very popular and handsome boy talking and laughing with a new girl at school who is also African American, very attractive, and whose skin is of a much darker tone. One girl remarks to the other, "What's he talking to her for? She's all black and ugly!" The other replies, " . . . hair all nappy lookin'."

Situation 2

At cheerleader tryouts, there are only two spots left. A light-skinned African American girl who attended all of the practices, showed up on time, and earned high marks on her evaluation has been selected over another girl who missed nearly a third of the practices, was late several times, but also received high marks on her evaluation. The girl who was *not* chosen remarks to her friends, "The only reason she got picked was because she's a red-bone."

Situation 3

Two girls who've been friends since elementary school and are now in junior high get into a very heated argument and begin to trade insults. One says, "At least I got good hair—ain't got that nappy stuff on my head like you." The other replies, "Well, I'd rather have my kind of hair than that white-girl hair that smells like a dog when it gets wet."

STAYING IN FOCUS ASSIGNMENT CARDS

Photocopy this page on card stock, then cut the cards apart (one card per participant).

SESSION 7: STAYING IN FOCUS

Think about what makes a person attractive.

SESSION 7: STAYING IN FOCUS

Think about what makes a person attractive.

SESSION 7: STAYING IN FOCUS

Think about what makes a person attractive.

SESSION 7: STAYING IN FOCUS

Think about what makes a person attractive.

SESSION 7: STAYING IN FOCUS

Think about what makes a person attractive.

SESSION 7: STAYING IN FOCUS

Think about what makes a person attractive.

72

From *Sisters of Nia: A Cultural Program to Empower African American Girls*, © 2008 by F. Z. Belgrave, V.R. Cherry, D.S. Butler, & T.G. Townsend. Champaign, IL: Research Press (www.researchpress.com; 1–800–517–2707)

Mirror, Mirror: What Do You Reflect? (Part 2)

If possible, invite a guest speaker to address the group as a part of this session. Speakers could include a licensed hairdresser specializing in the styling and care of natural hair, cosmetologist, or skin care consultant.

OBJECTIVES

- To continue open discussion of standards of beauty
- To continue to examine what can be done about putting down others
- To help the girls to gain an understanding of how their perceptions of their appearance affect their self-esteem
- To increase girls' appreciation of different forms of beauty

MATERIALS

CD player and CD of African percussion music

Water and plant for the *tambiko*

Easel pads and markers (one per *jamaa*)

Journals and copies of the Session 8 journal page (Appendix B, p. 141)

Pencils or pens

Session 8 *Staying in Focus* assignment cards

Snacks

73

PROCEDURE

Before the girls arrive, start the music. Continue to display the posters of the Nguzo Nane (Eight Principles) and Sisters of Nia Creed, along with the map of Africa.

Opening Rituals

- Turn off the music. Gather everyone together for the *durara umoja. Mzees* should spread themselves throughout the circle.
- Perform the *tambiko.*

Instruct the girls to get out their Staying in Focus assignment cards and go to their jamaas.

Jamaa Work

1. Ask for three volunteers. Have one post the *jamaa's* rules poster and the other two write the principle and proverb of the day, respectively.

   Nguzo/Principle: Heshema (Respect)

   Proverb: "Quarrels end, but words once spoken never die."

2. Have the girls practice saying the *nguzo* aloud. Discuss the meaning of the *nguzo* in relationship to the proverb. If necessary, explain that we have to be thoughtful about what we say because we cannot take back our words. Respecting ourselves and others requires not using words that hurt.

3. Let the group know that the session will continue to focus on what makes a person truly beautiful and on what participants can do to reduce put-downs and criticism based on physical appearance.

4. Discuss the last session's *Staying in Focus* assignment:

   "Think about what makes a person attractive."

   - Go around the circle and have each person quickly share her answer without discussion. Limit each participant to one trait or quality.
   - Write down all the girls' responses, then briefly discuss. Help the girls understand that, in addition to things like nice hair or skin, qualities such as kindness, respect for self

and others, and cleanliness are qualities that make a person attractive.

- Ask the girls how a person's perception of what makes someone attractive affects that person's self-esteem, then discuss.

- Ask the group if anyone helped someone else remember the assignment. If so, congratulate the girls for helping their "family" and recognize their efforts.

5. Hand out the journals, pencils or pens, and the journal page for the session. Read through the page and have the girls write down their answers for the first two questions.

6. Next ask the girls, "Now that we know more about some of the things that make us attractive, what can we do individually to solve the problems of put-downs and negative talk about others?" Provide one or two examples to get the brainstorming started. The strategies should be in the form of an "I" statement. For example:

- I will share what I've learned about the roots of the problem with my close friends.

- I will say at least one positive thing about another girl.

- I will focus on dealing with my own jealous (or other difficult) feelings.

    Even though participants need only two ideas to answer the third question, encourage them to come up with as many responses as they can. Write down their answers so that they have several from which to choose.

7. After you get at least five responses, stop the brainstorming and have the girls write their answers to the third question.

8. Collect the journals and pencils or pens and distribute the *Staying in Focus* assignment cards for the session:

    "Practice one of the strategies you listed to stop put-downs and negative talk about others."

    Read the instructions on the card and tell the girls that you want everyone to bring their card to the next session and be ready to share their answer. Continue to encourage them to help one another remember to bring their cards. Repeat the idea that this kind of help is a family responsibility.

If you are able to arrange for a speaker, the speaker may make her presentation at this point. Allow time at the end of the presentation for questions and answers.

Closing Rituals

- Get the whole group's attention, using the call and response method.
- Re-form the *durara umoja* and have everyone read the *Sisters of Nia Creed* together aloud.

Share the snacks. Mzees chat informally with the girls. Encourage everyone to help with clean-up.

$TAYING IN FOCU$ A$$IGNMENT CARD$

Photocopy this page on card stock, then cut the cards apart (one card per participant).

SESSION 8: STAYING IN FOCUS Practice one of the strategies you listed to stop put-downs and negative talk about others.	**SESSION 8: STAYING IN FOCUS** Practice one of the strategies you listed to stop put-downs and negative talk about others.
SESSION 8: STAYING IN FOCUS Practice one of the strategies you listed to stop put-downs and negative talk about others.	**SESSION 8: STAYING IN FOCUS** Practice one of the strategies you listed to stop put-downs and negative talk about others.
SESSION 8: STAYING IN FOCUS Practice one of the strategies you listed to stop put-downs and negative talk about others.	**SESSION 8: STAYING IN FOCUS** Practice one of the strategies you listed to stop put-downs and negative talk about others.

From *Sisters of Nia: A Cultural Program to Empower African American Girls*, © 2008 by F. Z. Belgrave, V.R. Cherry, D.S. Butler, & T.G. Townsend. Champaign, IL: Research Press (www.researchpress.com; 1–800–517–2707)

Taking Care of Yourself: Good Hygiene and Health

If possible, invite a guest speaker to address the group on topics like skin care, diet and nutrition, fitness, and other related topics.

OBJECTIVES

- To increase knowledge of the importance of good hygiene
- To encourage good hygiene habits
- To help girls understand the connection between good hygiene and health

MATERIALS

CD player and CD of African percussion music

Water and plant for the *tambiko*

Easel pads and markers (one per *jamaa*)

Journals and copies of the Session 9 journal page (Appendix B, p. 142)

Pencils or pens

Session 9 *Staying in Focus* assignment cards

Snacks

PREPARATION

Review the Hygiene and Health Questions on pages 83–85. If you wish, you can revise these questions to match topics covered in the school's family life education or health curriculum.

PROCEDURE

Before the girls arrive, start the music. Continue to display the posters of the Nguzo Nane (Eight Principles) and Sisters of Nia Creed, along with the map of Africa.

Opening Rituals

- Turn off the music. Gather everyone together for the *durara umoja*. *Mzees* should spread themselves throughout the circle.
- Perform the *tambiko*.

Instruct the girls to get out their Staying in Focus cards and go to their jamaas.

Jamaa Work

1. Ask for three volunteers. Have one post the *jamaa's* rules poster and the other two write the principle and proverb of the day, respectively.

   Nguzo/Principle: Nia (Purpose)

   Proverb: "If a child washes her hands, she could eat with kings."

2. Have the girls practice saying the *nguzo* aloud. Discuss the meaning of *nguzo* in relationship to the proverb. If necessary, explain that cleanliness and good hygiene are essential to good health and well-being.

3. Discuss the last session's *Staying in Focus* assignment:

   "Practice one of the strategies you listed to stop put-downs and negative talk about others."

   - Go around the circle and allow each person to quickly share her answer without discussion. Limit each girl to one strategy even if they practiced more than one. Congratulate them for their efforts, no matter how small.

   - Ask the group if anyone helped someone else remember the assignment. If so, congratulate the "family" and recognize their effort.

4. Introduce the topic of personal hygiene and health by asking the group how the principle and proverb might be related to

personal hygiene and self-image. Have participants give concrete examples. Discuss their responses.

5. Inform all of the *jamaas* that they will play a game in which each *jamaa* will work together to come up with answers to questions about personal hygiene. The goal is for each *jamaa* to truly work together.

Team-Building Activity: Personal Hygiene Game

In this activity, a mzee not assigned to a jamaa asks all of the jamaas a series of questions about personal hygiene. Another mzee can keep score.

Directions

1. Have each *jamaa* select a "spokeswoman."
2. Explain the following rules:

   - A *mzee* will read a number of questions aloud.
   - Each *jamaa* must work together to come up with an answer to each question within 15 seconds. The spokeswoman immediately raises her hand to signal that the group has an answer to the question.
   - The first *jamaa* to answer correctly receives five points.
   - If the question has several parts, one point is given for each part of the question answered correctly.
   - If an incorrect and/or incomplete answer is given, the question is passed on to the *jamaa* that had the second fastest response time.
   - If a question has more than one answer, one point is given for each additional correct answer.
   - If no answer is given in the allotted time, the *mzee* moves on to the next question.
   - The *jamaa* with the most points at the end of the questions wins.

   During the game, the mzees in each jamaa may help the group come to agreement on their answer but may not provide them with the answer. Mzees may give hints only if participants give no response following the reading of the question—in other words, only if the group is truly stumped.

---

6. In the individual *jamaas,* hand out the journals, pens or pencils, and journal page for the session. Discuss the questions on the page and have the girls answer them.

7. Collect the journals and pencils or pens and distribute the *Staying in Focus* assignment cards for the session:

"Practice one of the good hygiene and health behaviors you learned."

Read the instructions on the card and tell the girls that you want everyone to bring their card to the next session and be ready to share their answer. Encourage them to continue to work as a family.

If you are able to arrange for a speaker, the speaker may make her presentation at this point. Allow time at the end of the presentation for questions and answers.

Closing Rituals

- Get the whole group's attention, using the call and response method.

- Re-form the *durara umoja* and have everyone read the *Sisters of Nia Creed* together aloud.

Share the snacks. Mzees chat informally with the girls. Encourage everyone to help with clean-up.

HYGIENE AND HEALTH QUESTIONS

1. What is *hygiene? (Behaviors that ensure good health and cleanliness)*

2. Name three areas of the body that you associate with hygiene. *(Face, underarms, private area, feet)*

3. Is girls' hygiene different from boys' hygiene? *(Yes, girls have different hygiene needs—they may shave their legs and underarms, need feminine hygiene products for their periods, may need different products for hair, and so forth.)*

4. What is puberty? *(The period of time when a child's body begins to change into an adult's body)*

5. Name four changes that occur when a young girl goes through puberty. *(Physical changes include hormonal changes, breast development, weight gain, widening of hips, menstruation—your period begins—hair in pubic areas, and so forth. There are also many social and psychological changes during puberty.)*

6. Do all girls go through puberty at the same time? *(No, the age of puberty in girls varies from about age 8 to 13. All of us have different rates of maturing.)*

7. What is menstruation, or a "period"? *(Menstruation is a woman's monthly bleeding, also called a period. When you menstruate, your body is shedding the lining of the uterus, or womb.)*

8. Does the odor from your underarms change during puberty, and should you worry about it? *(Yes—underarm sweat glands become more active during puberty and produce a different odor. This is a natural part of puberty and not a cause for worry, although you may want to wear a deodorant.)*

9. What types of skin problems are related to puberty? *(Skin problems include acne—also called pimples or "zits." You can use special skin products to help control acne.)*

10. How often should you brush and floss your teeth? *(You should brush at least twice a day and floss at least once a day.)*

11. Is it necessary to get a new toothbrush at least every six months? *(Yes, your toothbrush does need to be replaced because it becomes worn and is not as effective.)*

12. How often should you take a shower? *(Daily)*

13. How often should you use deodorant? *(Daily)*

14. Name four things that you can do to take care of your hair. *(Washing regularly, conditioning, limiting use of chemicals and hair products that damage hair, combing and brushing)*

15. Name four items that you can use on your body that are directly related to hygiene. *(Soap, facial cleanser, deodorant, lotion, shampoo, and so on)*

16. When should you wash your hands? *(Before eating, after blowing your nose or sneezing, after using the bathroom)*

17. True or False? Skin is our first barrier of protection against germs. *(True)*

18. True or False? Germs can live under our fingernails and toenails. *(True)*

19. What areas are most susceptible to germs? *(Anywhere there are openings—nose, eyes, mouth)*

20. Is it OK to drop food and eat it, if not much time has passed? *(No, there are germs on the floor.)*

21. What are some of the things you should not share with friends? *(Makeup, comb, toothbrush, razor, and so forth)*

22. True or False? Many illnesses such as colds, the flu, and diarrhea can be prevented by frequently washing your hands with soap and water. *(True, frequently washing your hands, especially after using the bathroom and being in public places, can prevent illnesses.)*

23. If a friend falls and there is blood, what should you do? *(If possible, get an adult to help your friend.)*

24. Explain the expression "You are what you eat." *(Eating healthy and nutritious foods will result in better health and appearance.)*

25. When we talk about hygiene, we are concerned not with what you do to the outside of your body, but also what you put inside your body. Name three things that you put inside

the body that can affect you. *(Candy and sweets can affect teeth and gums; sodas and caffeine can contribute to skin problems; eating fresh vegetables and fruits can help you look better overall.)*

STAYING IN FOCUS ASSIGNMENT CARDS

Photocopy this page on card stock, then cut the cards apart (one card per participant).

SESSION 9: STAYING IN FOCUS

Practice one of the good hygiene and health behaviors you learned.

SESSION 9: STAYING IN FOCUS

Practice one of the good hygiene and health behaviors you learned.

SESSION 9: STAYING IN FOCUS

Practice one of the good hygiene and health behaviors you learned.

SESSION 9: STAYING IN FOCUS

Practice one of the good hygiene and health behaviors you learned.

SESSION 9: STAYING IN FOCUS

Practice one of the good hygiene and health behaviors you learned.

SESSION 9: STAYING IN FOCUS

Practice one of the good hygiene and health behaviors you learned.

From *Sisters of Nia: A Cultural Program to Empower African American Girls*, © 2008 by F. Z. Belgrave, V.R. Cherry, D.S. Butler, & T.G. Townsend. Champaign, IL: Research Press (www.researchpress.com; 1–800–517–2707)

Analyzing Media Messages

If you wish, supplement this activity by obtaining a copy of an age-appropriate DVD or videotape that depicts African American females in a negative way. Preview the material to be certain the content is appropriate and use it in the session to support the need for critical thinking about media messages.

OBJECTIVES

- To introduce girls to ways in which the media portray African American females
- To assist the girls in learning to critically examine myths and stereotypes of African American women presented in the media
- To further the girls' understanding of healthy relationships

MATERIALS

CD player and CD of African percussion music

Water and plant for the *tambiko*

Easel pads and markers (one per *jamaa*)

Journals and copies of the Session 10 journal page (Appendix B, p. 143)

Pencils or pens

Session 10 *Staying in Focus* assignment cards

Snacks

PROCEDURE

Before the girls arrive, start the music. Continue to display the posters of the Nguzo Nane (Eight Principles) and Sisters of Nia Creed, along with the map of Africa.

Opening Rituals

- Turn off the music. Gather everyone together for the *durara umoja. Mzees* should spread themselves throughout the circle.
- Perform the *tambiko.*

  Instruct the girls to get out their Staying in Focus assignment cards and go to their jamaas.

Jamaa Work

1. Ask for three volunteers. Have one post the *jamaa's* rules poster and the other two write the principle and proverb of the day, respectively.

   Nguzo/Principle: Kujichagulia (Self-Determination)

   Proverb: "The one who asks questions doesn't lose her way."

2. Have the girls practice saying the *nguzo* aloud. Discuss the meaning of the *nguzo* in relation to the proverb. If necessary, explain that taking care of yourself and meeting your goals involves asking questions and analyzing what you see and hear.

3. Discuss the last session's *Staying in Focus* assignment:

   "Practice one of the good hygiene and health behaviors you learned."

   - Ask the group: "With a show of hands and without saying what you did, who followed through on the assignment?"
   - Ask if anyone would like to share what they did. Don't discuss their answers. Simply thank them for sharing.
   - Continue to encourage participants' helping one another to remember the assignment. Recognize everyone's effort in following through: those who help, those who accept help or reminders, and those who previously needed reminding but now follow through on their own.

4. Introduce today's session by asking the group if they can remember the other sessions related to the principle of *Kujichagulia* (Self-Determination). If they can't remember, remind them that these sessions related to myths and misperceptions about Africa (Sessions 7 and 8). Ask the group, "What is a myth?" Tell them that in order to be able to identify information and images as myths, stereotypes, or misrepresentations, one must be able to think critically, just as they did in those earlier sessions.

5. Explain the concept of thinking critically. Ask the girls: "If consciousness is defined as an awareness or a kind of 'knowing' that is always with you in everything you do and say, then what is *critical consciousness?*"

6. After hearing from three or four girls, tell the group that we need to use this type of thinking to look beyond the appearance or first impression of something we see, read, experience, or hear. Critical consciousness means looking at how that particular thing we saw, read, experienced, or heard affects us as females and African Americans—socially, economically, and politically. It means listening with your "third ear" and seeing with your "third eye."

7. On the easel pad, write the following myths and stereotypes, one at a time.

    Myth 1: African American females are into money and material things.

    Myth 2: African American females are not very smart.

    Myth 3: In a relationship, it is okay for an African American woman to be called names and have her feelings hurt as long as the person apologizes and or buys gifts for her.

    Myth 4: African American females do not carry themselves in a ladylike manner (for example, they are loud).

    As you list each myth, ask the girls to give examples from magazines, television, films, music videos, and other media that include characters who fit these myths/stereotypes. Write down one or two examples for each myth.

    Simply list the examples. Keep the group focused and avoid allowing the girls to go off on tangents or give lengthy commentary on or criticism of the examples.

8. Hand out the journals, pencils or pens, and journal page for the session. Discuss the questions on the page and have the girls answer them.

9. Collect the journals, then distribute the *Staying in Focus* assignment cards for the session:

   "Practice thinking critically as you watch a television program or music video, listen to music, read a magazine, or experience some other media message."

   Read the instructions on the card. Tell the girls that you want everyone to bring their card and be ready to share their answer at the next session. Remind them that helping one another remember is a family responsibility.

10. Close by telling the group that, just as myths and negative stereotypes about Africa affect our self-concept and self-esteem, so do myths and stereotypes about African American women and girls. Despite the fact that these myths and stereotypes persist in the media, there are many intelligent, independent, courageous, beautiful-in-all-shades African American women in business, politics, the arts, and other areas of achievement.

Closing Rituals

- Get the whole group's attention, using the call and response method.
- Re-form the *durara umoja* and have everyone read the *Sisters of Nia Creed* together aloud.

   Share the snacks. Mzees chat informally with the girls. Encourage everyone to help with clean-up.

STAYING IN FOCUS ASSIGNMENT CARDS

Photocopy this page on card stock, then cut the cards apart (one card per participant).

SESSION 10: STAYING IN FOCUS

Practice thinking critically as you watch a television program or music video, listen to music, read a magazine, or experience some other media message.

SESSION 10: STAYING IN FOCUS

Practice thinking critically as you watch a television program or music video, listen to music, read a magazine, or experience some other media message.

SESSION 10: STAYING IN FOCUS

Practice thinking critically as you watch a television program or music video, listen to music, read a magazine, or experience some other media message.

SESSION 10: STAYING IN FOCUS

Practice thinking critically as you watch a television program or music video, listen to music, read a magazine, or experience some other media message.

SESSION 10: STAYING IN FOCUS

Practice thinking critically as you watch a television program or music video, listen to music, read a magazine, or experience some other media message.

SESSION 10: STAYING IN FOCUS

Practice thinking critically as you watch a television program or music video, listen to music, read a magazine, or experience some other media message.

From *Sisters of Nia: A Cultural Program to Empower African American Girls*, © 2008 by F. Z. Belgrave, V.R. Cherry, D.S. Butler, & T.G. Townsend. Champaign, IL: Research Press (www.researchpress.com; 1–800–517–2707)

Creativity: What I Can Offer

OBJECTIVES

- To assist the girls in identifying their creative thinking and leadership skills
- To increase bonding between girls from different *jamaas*

MATERIALS

CD player and CD of African percussion music

Water and plant for the *tambiko*

Easel pads and markers (one per *jamaa*)

Journals and copies of the Session 11 journal page (Appendix B, p. 144)

Pencils or pens

Session 11 *Staying in Focus* assignment cards

Snacks

PREPARATION

For the activity, put together a packet of items for each group of five or six girls (group size may vary according to the number of participants). The items in each packet must be identical in type and number. For example, a packet might include the following: 10 toothpicks, 10 drinking straws, 10 paper clips, 6 sturdy rubber bands, a piece of cloth (approximately 10 × 10 inches in size), a roll of tape, and a large envelope (to hold the other items).

PROCEDURE

Before the girls arrive, start the music. Continue to display the posters of the Nguzo Nane (Eight Principles) and Sisters of Nia Creed, along with the map of Africa.

Opening Rituals

- Turn off the music. Gather everyone together for the *durara umoja*. *Mzees* should spread themselves throughout the circle.
- Perform the *tambiko*.

Instruct the girls to get out their Staying in Focus assignment cards and go to their jamaas.

Jamaa Work

1. Ask for three volunteers. Have one post the *jamaa's* rules poster and the other two write the principle and proverb of the day, respectively.

   Nguzo/Principle: Kuumba (Creativity)

   Proverb: "If you are building a house and a nail breaks, do you stop building or do you change the nail?"

2. Have the girls practice saying the *nguzo* aloud. Discuss the meaning of the *nguzo* in relation to the proverb. Focus on the idea that there is usually more than one way to solve a problem.

3. Identify the session topic as recognizing creativity in oneself and others, then discuss the last session's *Staying in Focus* assignment:

   "Practice thinking critically as you watch a television program or music video, listen to music, read a magazine, or experience some other media message."

   - Tell the group to take a minute to think about what they have observed and what they think it means, then go around the circle and let them share their examples. If necessary, briefly clarify or summarize the interpretations of the examples the girls give.
   - Validate the girls' efforts in thinking more critically and encourage them to continue doing so.

- Recognize those who remembered to do the assignment and encourage group members to help one another remember future assignments.

4. Tell the group that, up to this point, they have mostly worked together as a *jamaa,* or family. Now they will be asked to go out into the larger *Sisters of Nia* community and work with those not in their own family. Openly recognize that it's okay if some people feel a little uncomfortable about doing this. Instruct them to abide by the rules of their *jamaa* and to remember and rely on what they have been learning and practicing over the past 10 sessions.

Team-Building Activity: Something from Nothing

Directions

1. Randomly form new groups of five or six members each (having the girls number off is a good strategy).

2. State clearly that the goal of the activity is for the members of each group to work together to invent, name, and create a six-second commercial for a "something." This invention can be as fanciful as they choose. Stress that this is not a competition between groups.

3. Explain the following rules:
   - Groups can use only those items given to them.
   - The items can be used in any way necessary.
   - Each group must work alone.
   - Groups should not open the packet of materials until told to do so.

4. Instruct the groups to spread out. Before you distribute the packets, remind the girls to keep them closed until you tell them to start. Hand out the packets.

5. Restate the goal of the activity. Ask if there are any questions. Remind participants that this is not a competition or contest, then instruct them to begin.

6. Give the groups 15 to 20 minutes, depending on time constraints, to develop their "something," name it, and present a commercial for it to the other groups. Everyone should participate in at least one of these roles.

7. Keep track of the time. Announce the time remaining at the midway point and, when the time expires, tell all of the groups to stop.

8. Ask for a group to volunteer to go first. The group should introduce their "something" and present their commercial (make sure they adhere to the six-second time limit).

9. Have the other groups give their presentations. Applaud each group for accomplishing their goal.

Processing the Activity

The girls should remain in their working groups during processing.

- Begin processing the activity by asking the groups if they achieved the goal or met the challenge they'd been given.

- Regardless of their reply, ask the groups to restate the goal or if they remember what the goal was. If necessary, restate the goal (to work together cooperatively).

- Finally, ask participants to relate the activity to the session's principle and proverb. Take two or three responses and then tell the girls to return to their original *jamaas*.

If you wish, you can save the inventions to display at the closing ceremony (Session 14).

5. When participants have joined their *jamaas,* congratulate them on working well in their new "communities." Hand out the journals, pencils or pens, and journal page for the session. Read the page aloud, discuss if necessary, and ask the girls to answer the questions.

6. Collect the journals and distribute the *Staying in Focus* assignment cards for the session. Read the instruction aloud:

"Be on the lookout for examples of creativity at school, at home, and in the community. Remember, there are different kinds of creativity."

Tell the girls that you want everyone to bring their card to the next session and be ready to share their answer. Remind them that doing so is a family responsibility.

Closing Rituals

- Get the whole group's attention, using the call and response method.
- Re-form the *durara umoja* and have everyone read the *Sisters of Nia Creed* together aloud.

    Share the snacks. Mzees chat informally with the girls. Encourage everyone to help with clean-up.

STAYING IN FOCUS ASSIGNMENT CARDS

Photocopy this page on card stock, then cut the cards apart (one card per participant).

SESSION 11: STAYING IN FOCUS Be on the lookout for examples of creativity at school, at home, and in the community. Remember, there are different kinds of creativity.	**SESSION 11: STAYING IN FOCUS** Be on the lookout for examples of creativity at school, at home, and in the community. Remember, there are different kinds of creativity.
SESSION 11: STAYING IN FOCUS Be on the lookout for examples of creativity at school, at home, and in the community. Remember, there are different kinds of creativity.	**SESSION 11: STAYING IN FOCUS** Be on the lookout for examples of creativity at school, at home, and in the community. Remember, there are different kinds of creativity.
SESSION 11: STAYING IN FOCUS Be on the lookout for examples of creativity at school, at home, and in the community. Remember, there are different kinds of creativity.	**SESSION 11: STAYING IN FOCUS** Be on the lookout for examples of creativity at school, at home, and in the community. Remember, there are different kinds of creativity.

From *Sisters of Nia: A Cultural Program to Empower African American Girls*, © 2008 by F. Z. Belgrave, V.R. Cherry, D.S. Butler, & T.G. Townsend. Champaign, IL: Research Press (www.researchpress.com; 1–800–517–2707)

African American Women in Leadership

If possible, invite an African American woman entrepreneur to speak to the group. This person might be a small business owner of a salon, beauty shop, store, consulting business, or medical practice.

OBJECTIVES

- To encourage the girls to become aware of African American women leaders in their family, home, and community
- To assist the girls in identifying and examining leadership qualities
- To encourage girls to develop their own leadership qualities

MATERIALS

CD player and CD of African percussion music

Water and plant for the *tambiko*

Easel pads and markers (one per *jamaa*)

Journals and copies of the Session 12 journal page (Appendix B, p. 145)

Session 12 *Staying in Focus* assignment cards

Pencils or pens

Snacks

PREPARATION

- For this session, compose and mail an invitation to the closing ceremony to the parents, guardians, or other adult caregivers of all of the girls who've attended at least half of the sessions. (A sample letter appears on page 106.) You can also invite other interested community members if you wish.

- For the activity, obtain carpet samples (or rubber mats) for about a third of the participants (for example, if you have 12 girls, obtain four carpet squares). The pieces should be large enough that all participants can fit on one but small enough so that it is difficult to do so (approximately 14 × 18 inches). Participants can balance on one foot, place one foot on top of one another, and hold onto each other to accomplish this.

PROCEDURE

Before the girls arrive, start the music. Continue to display the posters of the Nguzo Nane (Eight Principles) and Sisters of Nia Creed, along with the map of Africa.

Opening Rituals

- Turn off the music. Gather everyone together for the *durara umoja. Mzees* should spread themselves throughout the circle.
- Perform the *tambiko.*

    Instruct the girls to get out their Staying in Focus assignment cards and go to their jamaas.

Jamaa Work

1. Ask for three volunteers. Have one post the *jamaa's* rules poster and the other two write the principle and proverb of the day, respectively.

    Nguzo/Principles: Ujamaa (Cooperative Economics) and Nia (Purpose)

    Proverb: "If you educate a man, you educate an individual, but if you educate a woman, you educate a family."

2. Have the girls practice saying the *nguzo* aloud. Discuss the meaning of the *nguzo* in relation to the proverb. If necessary, point out that a woman has a great influence on everyone close

to her and is important to helping her family achieve their purpose.

3. Let the girls know that the topic of the session is African American women in leadership roles, then discuss the last session's *Staying in Focus* assignment:

"Be on the lookout for examples of creativity at school, at home, and in the community. Remember, there are different kinds of creativity."

Ask the girls to share one example of creativity they have seen. Try to cover examples in the family, at school, and in the community.

4. On the easel pad, write: "What is leadership?" Record the girls' responses and summarize by saying something like "True leadership is the encouragement and uplifting of others. It is teaching and sharing knowledge for the improvement and greater well-being of your family and community."

5. Ask the group to identify female leaders in their family, school, and community.

   - If the girls can think only of high-profile or famous people, cite some examples of leaders closer to home (for example, a grandmother raising a grandchild or an older teenager tutoring younger children in her community or caring for her younger siblings while a parent works). Do not write your own examples down.

   - If the group's examples do not include women entrepreneurs, clergy or church members, coaches or teachers, make a point to include them. Reaffirm the value and presence of leaders in our families and communities.

     You can refer to the African queens and leaders mentioned in Session 6 as examples of strong female leaders if you wish.

6. Next ask the girls to identify leadership qualities. Some of these might have come out when you defined *leadership* earlier in the session. If so, refer back to this list and circle the appropriate responses. Some of the qualities you want to be sure to include are courage, or doing what you know is right in spite of what others are doing; assertiveness (make sure the group

understands the difference between assertiveness and aggressiveness); and goal orientation or focus.

7. Let the girls know that they will be forming new groups of about 10 members each to participate in an activity. To form these groups, you can have the girls count off from 1 to 10.

Team-Building Activity: Underground Railroad

In this activity, a group (ideally 10 to 12 participants) must travel from a designated starting point to a designated destination. The challenge is that group members have limited resources to make the trip. Resources are represented by carpet squares, and the journey takes place from station to station. These stations are areas the same size as the carpet squares, marked with masking tape on the floor and approximately 36 inches apart. This distance is only a suggestion. The idea is to make it challenging but not impossible for the girls to move between stations. Also remember to closely monitor the activity at all times in order to ensure the physical and emotional safety of all participants.

Background

To get started, find out what the group knows about the Underground Railroad. If necessary, explain that the Underground Railroad was a system by which many people of African heritage escaped from slave states in the South to freedom in the North and Canada. They traveled at night with very little in the way of personal belongings and food. Abolitionists often assisted by establishing "stations" along the route where the escaping slaves could temporarily rest, receive food, and get useful information.

Directions

1. Explain to the group that they are a family traveling from one safe house or station to another and that everyone must go together, as a unit. No one may be left behind. Tell them there will be dangers on their journey as they travel but that they will be given a few resources for their journey.

2. Distribute carpet squares among the group and tell the group that these squares represent resources such as food, water, and one or two cherished possessions. These resources—along with their cooperation, trust in one another, determination, and faith—will aid them in making the journey.

3. Explain that the group must stand only on the carpet squares as they travel to their destination and that some part of their body must always be in contact with the squares. If a resource (square) is not being used (in physical contact with a group member), it will be taken away (forfeited) immediately, and the group will then have fewer resources to complete their trip. Should anyone step on the floor instead of on one of the squares at any time, the group will receive a consequence—for example, going back to the starting point, having one or more group members lose the ability to speak or see (if the latter, use a clean blindfold), or losing a resource (square).

In determining consequences, use your own judgment and let the activity's purpose guide you in your choices. For example, if you are trying to encourage leadership and vocal participation among shy and quiet group members, an effective consequence would be to take away the ability to speak from a few of the more vocal members.

4. Ask if there are any questions and answer them. However, do not offer information regarding possible consequences for stepping off a square. If asked, reply by saying something like "You never know what can happen."

5. Make sure everyone is behind the line of the starting point and that the next "station" or destination is well marked.

6. At this point, you can make up a story or scenario to make the activity even more interesting. For example, you could say that the group must go through a swamp and avoid the dangers there. Some rules must be observed: First, their feet must touch only the carpet squares as they move across the swamp. After all, swamps are homes to alligators, poisonous snakes, leeches, and so forth, so to step off the square can result in dire consequences. Second, they must demonstrate that they value their resources by maintaining physical contact with them at all times. In addition, they must always bring their resources (carpet squares) with them to the next station.

7. Have the group undertake their journey:

   - The group stands together at the starting point, holding their resources (carpet squares). Without stepping into the swamp, one of the group members tosses a carpet square onto the first station.

   - The entire group then moves onto the carpet square, bringing the remaining squares with them.

   - Once all of the group is on the first square at the first station, a group member tosses a carpet square onto the second station.

   - The group then moves together to the second station. Once at the second station, someone must retrieve the carpet square from the first station. (Typically, a group member reaches back to pick it up while other members provide support to prevent her from falling or stepping into the swamp, danger zone, etc.)

   - This process is repeated until the group reaches the end: "freedom."

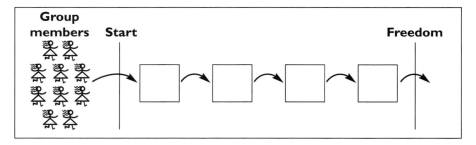

Processing the Activity

After the activity, reassemble the girls in the large group, then process the experience. Focus on feelings, self-discovery, and levels of cooperation. Sample questions include the following:

   - What was it like to work with people not in your *jamaa?*

   - Who learned something about themselves? What was it?

   - How did it feel when you first started out?

   - (*If consequences were given*) What were you thinking and feeling when _____ happened?

   - Why did/didn't you give up?

Ask the girls to relate the proverb and principle to the activity. Point out that our ancestors who braved the Underground Railroad faced death, beatings, and branding if they were caught. It was only because they were brave, determined, cooperative, creative, and intelligent that many were able to escape to freedom.

8. Have the girls return to their *jamaas* and, if appropriate, congratulate them on working well in the new groups. Discuss leadership and peer pressure:

   - Define *peer pressure* as pressure to do things or behave in a certain way to fit in and feel accepted by and part of a selected peer group. Point out that not all peer pressure is negative.

   - Ask the girls if they experienced peer pressure during the activity. Was it positive or negative?

   - Identify an example of positive peer pressure witnessed during the exercise. (One example would be someone trying to follow the *Sisters of Nia* creed and philosophy by being respectful of a peer.)

9. Hand out the journals, pencils or pens, and journal page for the session. Read through the journal page together and have the girls answer the questions. Close by having the girls read the following statements from their journal page aloud:

   "If the person you are following is not leading you in a POSITIVE and FORWARD direction, then you are not following a leader."

   "If you are not encouraging and elevating those around you and moving them in a POSITIVE and FORWARD direction, then you aren't being a leader."

10. Collect the journals and distribute the *Staying in Focus* assignment cards for the session. Read the instruction aloud:

    "Identify two African American women you admire."

    Tell the girls that you want everyone to bring their card to the next session and be ready to share their answer.

    If you are able to arrange for a speaker, the speaker may make her presentation at this point. Allow time at the end of the presentation for questions and answers.

Closing Ceremony Announcement

- Inform the girls that there are two sessions left in the program and that the last session will involve a closing ceremony to which parents, guardians, and other caregivers will be invited.

- Ask for two volunteers for this ceremony, one to explain and perform the *tambiko* for the parents and the other to write and present a brief essay on "What *Sisters of Nia* Means to Me."

- Let the girls know that you will be mailing an invitation to the closing ceremony to their parents, guardians, or other care-givers and that you want the girls to extend this invitation as well.

Closing Rituals

- Get the whole group's attention, using the call and response method.

- Re-form the *durara umoja* and have everyone read the *Sisters of Nia Creed* together aloud.

    Share the snacks. Mzees chat informally with the girls. Encourage everyone to help with clean-up.

STAYING IN FOCUS ASSIGNMENT CARDS

Photocopy this page on card stock, then cut the cards apart (one card per participant).

SESSION 12: STAYING IN FOCUS

Identify two African American women you admire.

SESSION 12: STAYING IN FOCUS

Identify two African American women you admire.

SESSION 12: STAYING IN FOCUS

Identify two African American women you admire.

SESSION 12: STAYING IN FOCUS

Identify two African American women you admire.

SESSION 12: STAYING IN FOCUS

Identify two African American women you admire.

SESSION 12: STAYING IN FOCUS

Identify two African American women you admire.

From *Sisters of Nia: A Cultural Program to Empower African American Girls*, © 2008 by F. Z. Belgrave, V.R. Cherry, D.S. Butler, & T.G. Townsend. Champaign, IL: Research Press (www.researchpress.com; 1–800–517–2707)

SAMPLE LETTER TO PARENTS AND GUARDIANS

[Your letterhead]

Date _____

Dear Parents and Guardians:

Please join us in recognizing your daughter for her accomplishments in completing the *Sisters of Nia* program. An awards ceremony will take place on _____ [date/time] at the following location:

_____

_____

All family members are invited, and refreshments will be served following the recognition ceremony.

Please RSVP no later than _____ [date] by calling _____ .

Sincerely,
Program Coordinator

SESSION 13

Education for Life

If possible, identify an African American female profes-
sional (an attorney, physician, business owner, college
professor, engineer, minister, or the like) to speak at this
session. Suggested topics include overcoming obstacles,
decision making, and setting goals.

OBJECTIVES

- To increase the girls' understanding of the importance of education
- To increase awareness of education as a way to further the well-being of African Americans
- To increase awareness of the importance of cultivating knowledge
- To increase awareness of the long-term consequences of not valuing education

MATERIALS

CD player and CD of African percussion music

Water and plant for the *tambiko*

Easel pads and markers (one per *jamaa*)

Journals and copies of the Session 13 journal page (Appendix B, p. 146)

Pencils or pens

Copies of the Education for Life Situations

Session 13 *Staying in Focus* assignment cards

PROCEDURE

Before the girls arrive, start the music. Continue to display the posters of the Nguzo Nane (Eight Principles) and Sisters of Nia Creed, along with the map of Africa.

Opening Rituals

1. Turn off the music. Gather everyone together for the *durara umoja*. *Mzees* should spread themselves throughout the circle.

2. Perform the *tambiko*.

   Instruct the girls to get out their Staying in Focus cards and go to their jamaas.

Jamaa Work

1. Choose three girls. Have one post the *jamaa's* rules poster and the other two write the principle and proverb of the day, respectively.

   Nguzo/Principle: Nia (Purpose)

   Proverb: "Lack of knowledge is darker than night."

2. Have the girls practice saying the *nguzo* aloud. Discuss the meaning of the *nguzo* in relation to the proverb. Focus on the idea that knowledge and education can help you achieve your purpose.

3. Tell girls that the topic of the session is the value of education, then discuss the last session's *Staying in Focus* assignment:

   "Identify two African American women you admire."

   Ask participants to let the group know which women they identified and describe what qualities they admire in these individuals. Recognize and praise those who remembered to do the assignment.

4. Explain that there are different kinds of knowledge. We learn many things in different ways. We learn how to read, play an instrument, solve problems peacefully, listen, play a sport, think critically, be an honest friend, overcome failure, and so forth. We learn by listening, watching or seeing, experiencing, and doing. Knowledge is vital to the advancement of African American people individually and as a whole.

5. Have the group brainstorm at least five ways we can cultivate our knowledge and, as they generate ideas, write the ideas on the easel pad. Sample responses include volunteer projects; tutoring others and receiving tutoring; study groups; book clubs; cultural programs; after-school programs; mentoring and being mentored; activities or programs affiliated with church, temple, or mosque; apprenticeships; and internships. (You may need to explain what apprenticeships and internships are.) Encourage the girls to name specific programs.

   If you wish, briefly describe one or two experiences as a preteen or teenager that furthered your own knowledge, such as participation in a tutoring/academic enrichment program or a vocational or volunteer project. Relate your experiences to the examples listed above.

6. Hand out the journals, pens or pencils, and journal page for the session. Read over the page and have the girls answer the questions.

7. Collect the journals and pens or pencils and explain that the girls will next have the opportunity to do some role plays relating to the importance of education.

Activity: Education for Life Role Plays

In this activity, mzees provide assistance as needed but allow the members of their jamaas to work out the details of the role plays as independently as possible.

Directions

1. Have each jamaa choose a role-play situation (or assign the situations, if you prefer).

2. Let the groups know that the skits are to be no longer than five minutes. The time limit must be observed to allow all of the *jamaas* equal time to perform and to keep the group focused.

3. *Mzees* instruct their jamaas to develop their role plays and rehearse them once or twice. Some *mzee* supervision may be required to ensure that developing the skit is a group process.

4. One of the senior *mzees* selects a *jamaa* to perform first. A *jamaa* member or *mzee* introduces the skit by describing the scenario, and the skit begins.

   The jamaas should perform their skits back to back, with no discussion or break in between. If there are four or more skits, make an exception; take a brief break for discussion midway through the presentations. Remember to enforce the five-minute time limit.

Processing the Activity

Reassemble the larger group and discuss the skits. Ask:

- Could anyone empathize or identify with the characters who made poor choices? If so, in what way? (*Mzees* may also respond to this question.)

- What would you have done differently to enable a positive outcome? (Direct this question first to the participants who portrayed characters who made poor choices, then to the entire group.)

   If appropriate, mzees may congratulate the jamaas on their ability to work together and resolve conflicts, as well as on the creativity and courage necessary to perform in front of a peer group.

8. Distribute the Staying in Focus assignment cards for the session:

   "What do you think of when you hear the word *faith?*"

   Remind the group that they should bring the cards to the next session and be ready to share their answers. Let them know that it is a family responsibility to help one another remember to do so.

9. Announce that the next session is the *Sisters of Nia* recognition ceremony and the final session and that each *jamaa* member will receive a certificate, her journal to take home, and a small gift to symbolize her achievement. Remind the girls that their parents and guardians, grandparents, and any other adult caregivers are invited. Ask the girls whether these people

have received invitations. If not, provide an additional copy of the letter.

If you are able to arrange for a speaker, the speaker may make her presentation at this point. Allow time at the end of the presentation for questions and answers.

Closing Rituals

- Get the whole group's attention, using the call and response method.
- Re-form the *durara umoja* and have everyone read the *Sisters of Nia Creed* together aloud.

  Share the snacks. Mzees chat informally with the girls. Encourage everyone to help with clean-up.

EDUCATION FOR LIFE SITUATIONS

Situation 1

Tiffany and Raven allow their friends to persuade them not to sign up for an after-school tutoring program because they'll miss out on _____ .

Characters: Tiffany, Raven, and a group of friends.

Situation 2

Angie is in the eighth grade and wants to become a pediatrician. While visiting one evening, a friend of her mother's who works as a nurse in the pediatrician's office invites Angie to volunteer at the office on Saturday mornings. Angie turns down the offer because she doesn't want to get up early on Saturdays.

Characters: Angie, her mother, and her mother's friend

Situation 3

It's the beginning of the school year. Looking over their class schedules, a group of five friends who are sophomores in high school discover that they all have a math teacher who is known to be "mean" (strict) and to "work you to death" (give a lot of homework). It is also known that this teacher's students do very well on the math portion of standardized tests such as the PSAT and SAT. Two of the girls decide that they're not going to "take any stuff from this teacher." They walk in, slam their books on their desk, sighing loudly, and utter phrases like "I don't wanna be here anyway!" and " . . . make me sick." They continue to do other things to disrupt the class. The other three girls reluctantly begin to join in.

Characters: Five friends and the teacher

From *Sisters of Nia: A Cultural Program to Empower African American Girls*, © 2008 by F. Z. Belgrave, V.R. Cherry, D.S. Butler, & T.G. Townsend. Champaign, IL: Research Press (www.researchpress.com; 1–800–517–2707)

Session 13 Handout

Situation 4

At basketball/cheerleading/step practice one afternoon, Aleisha, an average student, tells a few of her friends on the team that she can't stand her history class anymore because "It's so easy, it's boring." She goes on to say that since it's her last class of the day, she's just going to start leaving school early a couple of times a week. When a friend asks her about keeping up her grade-point average (all team members must maintain a 2.5 average), Aleisha replies she doesn't care because she get good grades (Cs) in her other classes.

Characters: Members of the team or squad and Aleisha

Situation 5

A successful African American female entrepreneur has volunteered to come to a local middle school to conduct a series of workshops for girls on topics such as earning and saving money, setting and working toward your goals, and so on. A teacher offers extra credit to a few students to attend and participate in the workshops. All of these students have at one time or another talked about the desire to own their own businesses, such as a hair salon or jewelry shop. At the workshops, the girls are inattentive and fail to participate fully.

Characters: Small group of girls, entrepreneur, and teacher

STAYING IN FOCUS ASSIGNMENT CARDS

Photocopy this page on card stock, then cut the cards apart (one card per participant).

SESSION 13: STAYING IN FOCUS

What do you think of when you hear the word *faith?*

SESSION 13: STAYING IN FOCUS

What do you think of when you hear the word *faith?*

SESSION 13: STAYING IN FOCUS

What do you think of when you hear the word *faith?*

SESSION 13: STAYING IN FOCUS

What do you think of when you hear the word *faith?*

SESSION 13: STAYING IN FOCUS

What do you think of when you hear the word *faith?*

SESSION 13: STAYING IN FOCUS

What do you think of when you hear the word *faith?*

From *Sisters of Nia: A Cultural Program to Empower African American Girls*, © 2008 by F. Z. Belgrave, V.R. Cherry, D.S. Butler, & T.G. Townsend. Champaign, IL: Research Press (www.researchpress.com; 1–800–517–2707)

116

Faith and Closing Ceremony

OBJECTIVES

- To help the girls gain an understanding of faith's role in achieving success
- To bring the program to a successful close

MATERIALS

CD player and CD of African percussion music

Water and plant for the *tambiko*

Easel pads and markers (one per *jamaa*)

Journals and copies of the Session 14 journal page (Appendix B, p. 147)

Pencils or pens

Copies of the Wheel of Sisterhood and Certificate of Recognition

Snacks (enough for participants and invited visitors)

PREPARATION

Make or purchase a small gift for each student. The gifts should be identical. An inexpensive ethnic bracelet or similar item would be appropriate.

PROCEDURE

Before the girls arrive, start the music. Continue to display the posters of the Nguzo Nane (Eight Principles) and Sisters of Nia Creed, along with the map of Africa.

Opening Rituals

- Turn off the music. Gather everyone together for the *durara umoja. Mzees* should spread themselves throughout the circle.
- Perform the *tambiko.*

  Instruct the girls to get out their Staying in Focus cards and go to their jamaas.

Jamaa Work

1. Instruct participants to go to their individual *jamaas*. Once in their *jamaas*, they should turn their chairs so that they face the front of the room.

2. Have one of the senior *mzees* call the entire group to order and announce that the proverb and principle of the day will be discussed in the larger community. Select two participants, one to write the principle and proverb and another to read them aloud to the group.

   Nguzo/Principle: Imani (Faith)

   Proverb: "Patience can cook a stone."

   Encourage the girls to recite the *nguzo* and proverb together, then discuss the meaning of the proverb (with patience and restraint, you can solve even the most difficult problems).

3. Have another *mzee* come forward and continue the discussion by asking the girls: "What do you think of when you hear the word *faith?*"

   At this point, mzees should be careful not to relate the nguzo (faith) to religion. In other words, stick to the idea of a higher spiritual belief without relating it to specific religious institutions.

4. Have another *mzee* close the discussion with a definition of *faith*. A sample definition is "Faith is more than hoping or wishing. It means strongly believing and working hard to

live what you believe and to endure or continue in spite of whatever obstacles you may face."

5. Have the girls break into their *jamaas*. At this point, hand out the journals, pencils or pens, and the session's journal page, but do not discuss the questions at this time.

6. Next hand out copies of the Wheel of Sisterhood. Explain:

    "This is our last session, and we want to leave you and have you leave one another with a positive word."

    - To do this, each girl writes her name in the space provided and then passes her sheet to the person on her right. (Everyone does this at the same time.)

    - The person receiving the paper writes a positive word or two that they think describes that person on one of the spokes.

    - Then, simultaneously, everyone again passes the paper to the right.

    - The next person does the same on a blank spoke and so on.

    - Continue with each person's writing a descriptive word or two until the paper comes back to its owner.

    - At this point, each participant's wheel should have a positive word or two from each of her jamaa members and *mzees.*

Closing Ceremony

1. A senior *mzee* announces that the closing ceremony will now begin. Have the girl who volunteered at the last session explain and perform the *tambiko.*

2. Have the second volunteer make her presentation on the topic "What *Sisters of Nia* Means to Me."

3. Have all the *mzees* stand. A *mzee* from each *jamaa* comes to the front with the certificates. (The other *mzees* remain with the *jamaas* to distribute the gifts.)

4. Have a senior *mzee* say: "These gifts symbolize how far you've come on your journey as a *Sister of Nia.*"

5. *Mzees* take turns calling individual *jamaa* members up front to receive their certificates. As each girl comes to the front, a *mzee* greets the girl with "Welcome, sister. You have come a long

way." When the girl returns to her *jamaa,* another *mzee* presents her with a small gift.

Closing Rituals

> *If you wish, you can have parents and other invited guests participate in the durara umoja.*

- After the certificates and gifts have been presented, call the group to order using the call and response method and form the *durara umoja.*

- At this point, *mzees* from each *jamaa* may briefly identify a "gift" they have received from the girls. It may be something they learned or perhaps a new experience or insight.

- Close by encouraging the girls to continue to remember and practice what they've learned and by reciting the *Sisters of Nia Creed* together.

> *Share the snacks. Mzees chat informally with the girls and their parents or caregivers. Participants help with clean-up.*

WHEEL OF SISTERHOOD

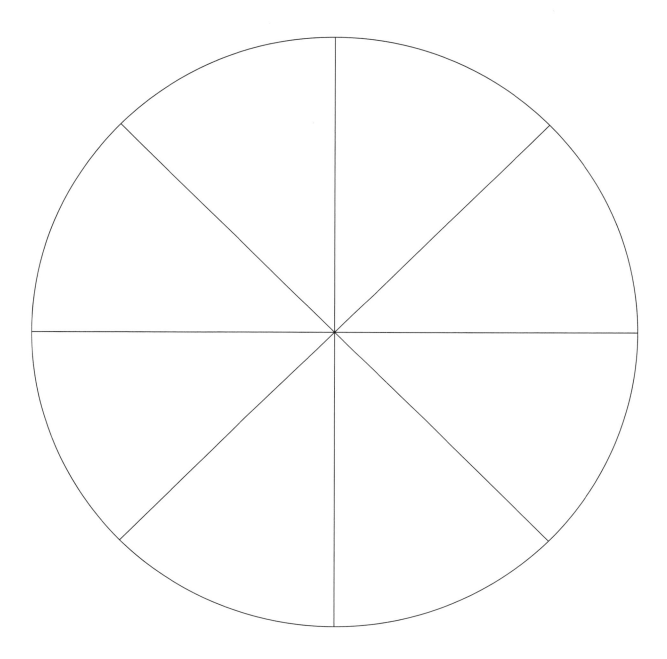

CERTIFICATE OF ACHIEVEMENT

This certifies that

_____

is awarded special recognition for her commitment
to cultural enrichment and participation in

SISTERS OF NIA

Given at _____ this _____ day of _____

_____
Mzee

_____
Program Coordinator

Session 14 Handout

From *Sisters of Nia: A Cultural Program to Empower African American Girls*, © 2008 by F. Z. Belgrave, V.R. Cherry, D.S. Butler, & T.G. Townsend. Champaign, IL: Research Press (www.researchpress.com; 1–800–517–2707)

Kwanzaa

OBJECTIVES

- To familiarize girls with a cultural celebration of African Americans
- To provide the girls an opportunity to participate in a Kwaanza celebration

MATERIALS

CD or audiotape of African percussion music

Water and plant for the *tambiko*

Copies of the Kwanzaa handout *(optional)*

Craft materials for the gift-making activity (jewelry, soaps, etc.)

Snacks

PREPARATION

Obtain and arrange the following Kwanzaa symbols and decorations:

Mkeka—a straw mat at least 2 x 3 feet

Kinara—a candle holder that will hold seven candles

Mishumaa Saba—three red, one black, and three green candles for the *Kinara*

Muhindi—ears of dried corn

Kikombe cha Umoja—a cup or goblet (Unity Cup)

Mazao—a basket of fruits and vegetables

Place the *mkeka* on a low table or the floor. Additional decorations may include Kente cloth, mud cloth, and other fabrics of African design, books about Kwanzaa, African art, and so forth.

PROCEDURE

Before the girls arrive, start the music. Continue to display the posters of the Nguzo Nane (Eight Principles) and Sisters of Nia Creed, along with the map of Africa.

Opening Rituals

- Turn off the music. Gather everyone together for the *durara umoja*. Staff should spread themselves throughout the circle.
- Perform the *tambiko*.

Group Discussion

1. Introduce Kwanzaa by asking the girls if any of them have attended a Kwanzaa celebration and/or can tell the group what it is. If no one responds, ask them to guess or tell what they think it is.
2. If you wish, distribute copies of the Kwanzaa handout. Explain the history and symbolism of Kwanzaa. It is important that the girls understand that it is not a religious observance and does not replace Christmas or other religious holidays for those who observe it.
3. Lead the group through the lighting of all of the *Mishumaa Saba* (candles). Girls from each *jamaa* may be called to light a candle.

Gift Making

1. Have the girls go to their *jamaas*. Tell the girls, if they don't already know, that one of the traditions of Kwanzaa is making gifts to give to others.
2. Pass out the craft supplies and have the girls make the gifts.

Closing Rituals

- Get the whole group's attention, using the call and response method.

- Re-form the *durara umoja* and have everyone read the *Sisters of Nia Creed* together aloud.

  Share the snacks. Mzees chat informally with the girls. Encourage everyone to help with clean-up.

KWANZAA

Kwanzaa is an African and African American holiday, celebrated from December 26 through January 1, that celebrates family, community and culture. It was created in 1966 by Dr. Maulana Karenga, a professor in the Department of Black Studies at California State University in Long Beach, California. The rituals of Kwanzaa are rooted in the first harvest celebrations of Africa. Kwanzaa is a cultural holiday, not a religious one, and is therefore available to and practiced by Africans and African Americans of all religious faiths.

KWANZAA SYMBOLS AND THEIR MEANINGS

Mazao (the crops)
   African harvest and the rewards of productive and collective labor

Mkeka (the mat)
   Tradition, history, and the foundation on which to build

Kinara (the candle holder)
   African roots, our ancestors from Africa

Muhindi (the corn)
   Children and our future

Mishumaa Saba (the Seven Candles)
   Representing the Nguzo Saba, the Seven Principles that African and African American people are urged to live by

Kikombe cha Umoja (the Unity Cup)
   The principle and practice of unity, which make all else possible

Zawadi (gifts)
   The labor and love of parents and the commitments made and kept by children

From *Sisters of Nia: A Cultural Program to Empower African American Girls,* © 2008 by F. Z. Belgrave, V.R. Cherry, D.S. Butler, & T.G. Townsend. Champaign, IL: Research Press (www.researchpress.com; 1–800–517–2707)

Optional Session Handout

Appendix A

Research Support

What is the evidence that the *Sisters of Nia* curriculum will result in the objectives outlined previously? More than 300 girls 10 to 14 years of age have participated in the *Sisters of Nia* curriculum or a similar cultural program in Washington, D.C., and Richmond, Virginia. More than 200 others have participated in comparison group activities that have allowed us to determine whether or not participating in the cultural program produces the desired changes. Two outcome studies show that participants in the cultural curriculum have improved in targeted outcomes.

One study evaluated the effectiveness of the cultural curriculum for strengthening resiliency among African American preadolescent girls (Belgrave, Chase-Vaughn, Gray, Addison, & Cherry, 2000). Participants were African American girls ages 10 to 12 who resided in an urban community in Washington, D.C. Fifty-five girls participated in the cultural curriculum, and 92 girls were in a comparison group. Girls in the comparison group were exposed to guest speakers and recreational activities but did not receive the cultural curriculum.

Girls in the cultural curriculum met once a week for two hours over a period of four months. They were engaged in exercises and activities designed to increase feelings of self-worth, Africentric values, and ethnic identity. Analyses involved comparing participants in the cultural group with participants in the comparison group on posttest measures while holding pretest scores constant. Findings showed that participants in the cultural curriculum group scored significantly higher on measures of ethnic identity, Africentric values, and self-concept than participants in the comparison group at posttest (see Figure 1).

Figure 1

Posttest Scores for Cultural Variables for Cultural and Comparison Groups

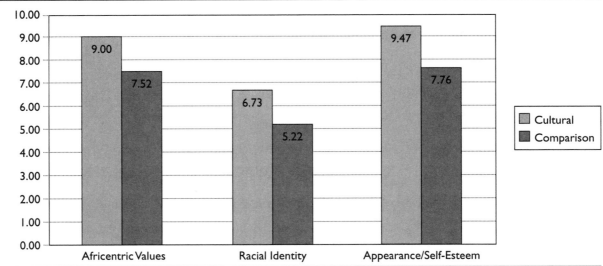

A second study evaluated the effectiveness of the *Sisters of Nia* curriculum for increasing cultural values and beliefs, including ethnic identity and gender roles, and for decreasing relational aggression among a sample of girls in Richmond, Virginia (Belgrave, 2002). Fifty-nine girls ages 11 to 12 years of age participated in 15 two-hour cultural curriculum sessions or in tutoring sessions (comparison group). Measures of ethnic identity, gender roles, and relational aggression were administered to both groups at the beginning and the end of the intervention.

The findings showed significant differences in ethnic identity and marginally significant increases in androgynous gender role beliefs for girls in the cultural curriculum group but not the comparison group at posttest (see Figures 2 and 3). Androgynous

Figure 2

Posttest Scores for Participants in *Sisters in Nia* and Comparison Groups

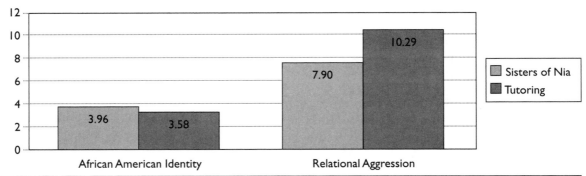

Appendix A

Figure 3

Percentage of Participants with Androgynous Gender Role Beliefs at Pretest and Posttest for *Sisters of Nia* and Tutoring Participants

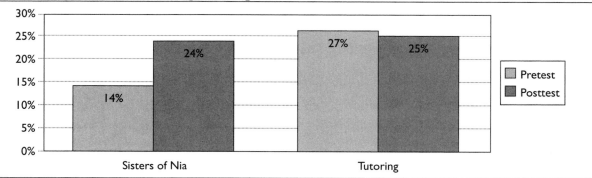

gender role beliefs endorse both feminine and masculine gender roles. These beliefs are linked to several favorable outcomes for female adolescents, among them higher school achievement, higher life-course expectations, and less-risky sexual behaviors. Also, participants in the *Sisters of Nia* group decreased in relational aggression (verbal insults, gossiping, putting others down, and so forth), but that was not the case for the comparison group.

REFERENCES

Belgrave, F. Z., Chase-Vaughn, G., Gray, F., Addison, J. D., & Cherry, V. R. (2000). The effectiveness of a culture- and gender-specific intervention for increasing resiliency among African American preadolescent females. *Journal of Black Psychology, 26,* 133–147.

Belgrave, F. Z. (2002). Relational theory and cultural enhancement interventions for African American adolescent girls. *Public Health Reports, 117,* S76–S81.

APPENDIX B

Sisters of Nia Journal

SISTERS OF NIA JOURNAL

My Name

_____

My *Jamaa* Name

_____

My *Mzee's* Name

_____

Date

_____

SISTERS OF NIA CREED

- We will not speak negatively of, ridicule, or belittle our sisters.

- We will work to help each other have positive feelings about who we are by complimenting each other.

- We accept responsibility for what we do, who we are, and what we can become.

- We will trust our inner voices.

NIA (PURPOSE)

Before shooting, one must aim.

1. Write the names of the members of your *jamaa*.

2. Write down two things you can contribute to your *jamaa*.

UJIMA (TEAMWORK)

Show me your friend, and I will show you your character.

1. **What is a relationship?**

2. **List at least two types of relationships.**

3. **A *sister-friend* is a female friend you can count on. She is someone who is helpful, honest, encouraging, a good listener, unselfish, and so on. What makes you a good sister-friend?**

Session 3

UJIMA (TEAMWORK)
UMOJA (UNITY)

When spiderwebs unite, they can tie up a lion.

1. List at least three elements of a healthy relationship.

2. What does it mean to be a member of the *Sisters of Nia* or a sister-friend?

From *Sisters of Nia: A Cultural Program to Empower African American Girls,* © 2008 by F. Z. Belgrave, V.R. Cherry, D.S. Butler, & T.G. Townsend. Champaign, IL: Research Press (www.researchpress.com; 1–800–517–2707)

KUJICHAGULIA (SELF-DETERMINATION)

She who does not cultivate her fields will die of hunger.

What do you think about Africa?

1. I think Africa is . . .

2. Africa is a place where . . .

3. African people are . . .

4. In the past, Africa was . . .

5. Africans and African Americans are . . .

6. I would (or would not) like to visit Africa because . . .

KUJICHAGULIA
(SELF-DETERMINATION)

A people without knowledge of its history is like a tree without roots.

1. In the past, I thought Africa was . . .

NOW I KNOW THAT IT IS . . .

2. In the past, I thought African people were . . .

NOW I KNOW THAT THEY ARE . . .

HESHEMA (RESPECT)

One who defames another's character also defames her own.

1. Have you ever had a conflict with someone about your own or their appearance? What was the conflict about?

2. How did you handle the conflict? How could it have been handled better?

3. Why do girls, even good friends, put down and harshly criticize each other?

HESHEMA (RESPECT)

Quarrels end, but words once spoken never die.

1. What are two things that YOU think make a person attractive?

2. Does your behavior affect whether or not you're an attractive person?

3. What are two things YOU can do about the problem of put-downs and negative talk about others?

NIA (PURPOSE)

If a child washes her hands, she could eat with kings.

1. Two things I do now to practice good hygiene are . . .

2. Something I learned about good hygiene is that I can . . .

KUJICHAGULIA (SELF-DETERMINATION)

The one who asks questions doesn't lose her way.

1. What was happening to the females in the situations we discussed?

2. How do you feel about it?

3. What message does it send?

4. Does this message fit in with the *Sisters of Nia Creed*?

5. What would you do differently?

From *Sisters of Nia: A Cultural Program to Empower African American Girls,* © 2008 by F. Z. Belgrave, V.R. Cherry, D.S. Butler, & T.G. Townsend. Champaign, IL: Research Press (www.researchpress.com; 1–800–517–2707)

KUUMBA (CREATIVITY)

If you are building a house and a nail breaks, do you stop building or do you change the nail?

1. What was the goal of the activity?

2. Did your group accomplish its goal? Why? Why not?

3. What are your feelings about what your group did?

4. Why is it important to focus on what you have to work with instead of on what you're lacking?

From *Sisters of Nia: A Cultural Program to Empower African American Girls,* © 2008 by F. Z. Belgrave, V.R. Cherry, D.S. Butler, & T.G. Townsend. Champaign, IL: Research Press (www.researchpress.com; 1–800–517–2707)

Session 11

UJAMAA
(COOPERATIVE ECONOMICS)
NIA (PURPOSE)

If you educate a man, you educate an individual,
but if you educate a woman, you educate a family.

1. What are two qualities of a positive leader?

2. What does POSITIVE peer pressure feel like?

3. Name two things you can do to be a positive leader.

REMEMBER

- If the person you are following is not leading you in a POSITIVE and FORWARD direction, then you are not following a leader.

- If you are not encouraging and elevating those around you, moving them in a POSITIVE and FORWARD direction, then you aren't being a leader.

From *Sisters of Nia: A Cultural Program to Empower African American Girls,* © 2008 by F. Z. Belgrave, V.R. Cherry, D.S. Butler, & T.G. Townsend. Champaign, IL: Research Press (www.researchpress.com; 1–800–517–2707)

NIA (PURPOSE)

Lack of knowledge is darker than night.

1. What are two ways to cultivate your knowledge in school?

2. What are two ways to cultivate your knowledge in the community?

IMANI (FAITH)

Patience can cook a stone.

1. **What does FAITH mean to you?**

2. **Do you think the proverb is true? Why or why not?**

REMEMBER

Being a *Sister of Nia* begins with you!

APPENDIX C

Program Posters

SISTERS OF NIA CREED

We will not speak negatively of, ridicule, or belittle our sisters.

We will work to help each other have positive feelings about who we are by complimenting each other.

We accept responsibility for what we do, who we are, and what we can become.

We will trust our inner voices.

From *Sisters of Nia: A Cultural Program to Empower African American Girls,* © 2008 by F. Z. Belgrave, V.R. Cherry, D.S. Butler, & T.G. Townsend. Champaign, IL: Research Press (www.researchpress.com; 1–800–517–2707)

NGUZO NANE

EIGHT PRINCIPLES FOR AFRICAN AMERICAN LIVING

1. Nia: Purpose
2. Ujima: Collective Work and Responsibility (Teamwork)
3. Umoja: Unity
4. Kujichagulia: Self-Determination
5. Heshema: Respect
6. Kuumba: Creativity
7. Ujamaa: Cooperative Economics
8. Imani: Faith

From *Sisters of Nia: A Cultural Program to Empower African American Girls*, © 2008 by F. Z. Belgrave, V.R. Cherry, D.S. Butler, & T.G. Townsend. Champaign, IL: Research Press (www.researchpress.com; 1–800–517–2707)

NGUZO/PRINCIPLE

NIA (PURPOSE)

NGUZO/PRINCIPLE

UJIMA (TEAMWORK)

NGUZO/PRINCIPLE

UMOJA (UNITY)

NGUZO/PRINCIPLE

KUJICHAGULIA
(SELF-DETERMINATION)

From *Sisters of Nia: A Cultural Program to Empower African American Girls*, © 2008 by F. Z. Belgrave, V.R. Cherry, D.S. Butler, & T.G. Townsend. Champaign, IL: Research Press (www.researchpress.com; 1-800-517-2707)

NGUZO/PRINCIPLE

HESHEMA (RESPECT)

NGUZO/PRINCIPLE

KUUMBA (CREATIVITY)

NGUZO/PRINCIPLE

UJAMAA
(COOPERATIVE ECONOMICS)

From *Sisters of Nia: A Cultural Program to Empower African American Girls*, © 2008 by F. Z. Belgrave, V.R. Cherry, D.S. Butler, & T.G. Townsend. Champaign, IL: Research Press (www.researchpress.com; 1–800–517–2707)

NGUZO/PRINCIPLE

IMANI (FAITH)

Glossary

Durara umoja *(doo-RAH-rah oo-MOH-jah)*
Unity circle, symbolizing togetherness and support of one another

Heshema *(he-SHEM-mah)*
Respect (program principle)

Imani *(ee-MAH-nee)*
Faith (program principle)

Jamaa *(JAH-mah)*
Family or group

Kikombe cha Umoja *(kee-KOHM-bay cha oo-MOH-jah)*
The Unity Cup used in the Kwanzaa celebration

Kinara *(kee-NAH-rah)*
Candle holder used in the Kwanzaa celebration

Kujichagulia *(koo-jee-chah-goo-LEE-ah)*
Self-determination (program principle)

Kuumba *(koo-OOM-bah)*
Creativity (program principle)

Mazao *(mah-ZAH-oh)*
Fruits and vegetables (crops) used in the Kwanzaa celebration

Mishumaa Saba *(mee-shoo-MAH SAH-bah)*
Seven candles representing the seven principles *(Nguzo Saba)* in the Kwanzaa celebration

Mkeka *(m-KAY-kah)*
Mat used in the Kwanzaa celebration

Muhindi *(moo-HEEN-dee)*
Corn used in the Kwanzaa celebration

Mzee *(m-ZAY)*
Respected elder

Nguzo Nane *(n-GOO-zoh NAH-nay)*
Eight *(Nane)* Principles *(Nguzo)* of African American living on which the *Sisters of Nia* program is based

Nguzo Saba *(n-GOO-zoh SAH-bah)*
Seven *(Saba)* Principles *(Nguzo)* of Kwanzaa

Nia *(NEE-ah)*
Purpose (a program principle)

Tambiko *(tahm-BEE-koh)*
Libations, or the pouring of water into the earth in memory of ancestors

Ujamaa *(oo-JAH-mah)*
Cooperative economics (program principle)

Ujima *(oo-JEE-mah)*
Collective work and responsibility (program principle)

Umoja *(oo-MOH-jah)*
Unity (program principle)

Zawadi *(zah-WAH-dee)*
Gifts given as part of the Kwanzaa celebration

Suggested Resources

African American Adolescent Girls

Carroll, R. *Sugar in the Raw: Voices of Young Black Girls in America.* New York: Random House, 1997.

Davis-Thompson, E. *Raising Up Queens: Loving Our Daughters Loud and Strong.* Philadelphia: Innisfree Press, 2000.

Ferebee, J. *Got It Goin' On: Power Tools for Girls,* 2004. (Available from Got It Goin' On, 1221 Massachusetts Ave. N.W., Ste. 609, Washington, DC 20005–5315 or www.janiceferebee.com)

Hrabowski, F.A., Maton, K.I., Greene, M.L., and Greif, G.L. *Overcoming the Odds: Raising Academically Successful African American Young Women.* New York: Oxford University Press, 2004.

Leadbetter, B.J., Ross, R., and Way, N.C. *Urban Girls Revisited.* New York: New York University Press, 2007.

Leadbetter, B.J., and Way, N.C. *Urban Girls: Resisting Stereotypes, Creating Identities.* New York: New York University Press, 1996.

Sisters Helping Sisters: The Wheeler Avenue Baptist Church Girls' Rites of Passage Program. Chicago: African American Images, 1998.

Stevens, J. *Smart and Sassy: The Strengths of Inner City Black Girls.* New York: Oxford University Press, 2002.

Valerius, D.S. *Souls of Black Girls* (Documentary), 2006. (Available from www.soulsofblackgirls.com)

African Americans and Africa

Appiah, K.A. *In My Father's House: Africa in the Philosophy of Culture.* New York: Oxford University Press, 1992.

Dodson, H. *Jubilee: The Emergence of African American Culture.* Washington, DC: National Geographic Books, 2003.

Perry, T., Steele, C., and Hilliard, A. *Young, Gifted, and Black: Promoting High Achievement Among African-American Students.* Boston: Beacon Press, 2003.

van Sertima, I. *Black Women in Antiquity.* New Brunswick, NJ: Transaction Publishers, 1997.

About the Authors

FAYE Z. BELGRAVE is a professor of psychology and director of the Center for Cultural Experiences in Prevention at Virginia Commonwealth University. Dr. Belgrave has implemented and/or evaluated programs for African American youth for over 15 years. Her programs and research have always considered the role of culture and context in preventing substance abuse, early and risky sexual activity, and other problem behaviors. Dr. Belgrave has received national awards from the Association of Black Psychologists, the American Psychological Association, and the Substance Abuse and Mental Health Services Administration for her work on behalf of ethnic minority youth. Dr. Belgrave received a Ph.D. from the University of Maryland, a master's degree from the University of Nebraska–Lincoln, and a bachelor of science degree from North Carolina Agricultural and Technical State University. She is the parent of Angela and Alex.

VALERIE RAWLS CHERRY has served as principal mental health consultant to the U.S. Department of Labor's Job Corps program for the past 11 years. In this capacity, she provides technical assistance, training, program development, and site reviews for health and wellness programs at over 120 Job Corps centers in the United States and Puerto Rico. Dr. Cherry is a licensed clinical psychologist with over 20 years of clinical and research experience working with at-risk youth and their families. Her experience over the years has ranged from serving as director for programs funded by the Center for Substance Abuse Prevention to director of an adolescent treatment facility. Dr. Cherry's areas of interest are prevention, gender differences, and cultural competency. Dr. Cherry is married, with one son, Jamal Malik.

DEBORAH S. BUTLER is currently a project director at the Center for Cultural Experiences in Prevention at Virginia Commonwealth University. The project is devoted to the study of cultural, family, and community factors that affect substance use among African American youth. Ms. Butler was the senior prevention specialist responsible for implementing *Sisters of Nia* with several hundred girls in the Richmond metro area. Prior to joining Virginia Commonwealth University, she worked in the Washington, D.C., area, developing and implementing prevention programs as a counselor for a youth program and as a team trainer for substance abuse prevention programming. Ms. Butler received her bachelor of science degree in biology from Eastern New Mexico University and a master's degree in interdisciplinary studies–psychology and education from Virginia Commonwealth University. She is the parent of three children, Melissa, Micah, and Ivan.

TIFFANY G. TOWNSEND received her Ph.D. in clinical psychology with a minor in child/community psychology from George Washington University in 1998. She is currently on the faculty of Georgetown University's Department of Psychiatry. Her clinical and research activities focus on the implementation of community-based research and intervention programs to enhance the health and psychosocial functioning of ethnic minority children and their families. Currently, Dr. Townsend is principal investigator on the I.S.I.S. project, funded by the Substance Abuse and Mental Health Services Administration's Center for Substance Abuse Prevention. This program is aimed at HIV and substance abuse prevention among African American adolescent girls in southwest Philadelphia. She is also the principal investigator for the Aza Sisters program, funded by the National Institutes of Health to focus on HIV prevention among girls who have had traumatic life circumstances.